From the Chariot
YOGA WISDOM FOR MODERN LIVING

NAND NARINE

Copyright © 2012 Nand Narine in partnership with BOBAIR MEDIA INC.

Published by Nand Narine through BOBAIR MEDIA INC.
Produced in Edmonton, Alberta.

ACKNOWLEDGMENTS
To the following friends and colleagues. For your enthusiasm, hard work and creativity.

Design and graphics by Jody Youngren
Photography by Mike Yarske
Model: Chantele Theroux

Thank you.

This book is dedicated
to the loving memory of my parents
and my family and friends
for their support and assistance
during wonderful times and challenging moments.

Shanti Om

CONTENTS

Introduction – ix

ONE

The Playing Field – 1

TWO

Power of the Senses – 13

THREE

Non-Attachment to the Fruits of Action – 25

FOUR

Divine Manifestations – 33

FIVE

The Inside Journey – 43

SIX

The Practice of Yoga – 53

SEVEN

Free Will and Individual Choice – 69

EIGHT

Managing the Gates – 79

NINE

From the Heart – 89

TEN

Source Energy – 99

ELEVEN

Divine Vision – 107

TWELVE

Bhakti Yoga – 117

THIRTEEN

Divinity Everywhere – 127

FOURTEEN

The Three Gunas – 137

FIFTEEN

Prana Vayus and Digestive Fire – 149

SIXTEEN

The Dark Side – 159

SEVENTEEN

Spiritual Science of Food – 171

EIGHTEEN

The Victorious Connection – 181

Index
Recommended Reading List
Mantras and Kirtans
Bibliography, Permissions

> The moment you have in your heart
> this thing called Love,
> and you feel the depth, the delight and the ecstasy of it,
> your world, as you know it, is transformed.
> – Jiddu Krishnamurti

INTRODUCTION

The need to connect with Divine Energy exists in every human being. In a technologically advanced world with a fast paced, multitasking culture, the challenge is to establish and maintain that connectivity. The mechanism used to make this connection varies considerably from one person to the other, and from one stage of life to the next. Nevertheless, we are all spiritual seekers of one kind or another.

We have heard this for many years from the various priests, yogis, saints and sages. In the academic arena, Abraham Maslow brought this concept to our attention in his 1943 Hierarchy of Needs Model. After we have fulfilled our physiological, safety, social and self-esteem needs, we move on to the pursuit of self- actualization. Clayton

Alderfer later expanded this approach in his 1969 *ERG Theory (Existence, Relatedness and Growth)*. He combined the self-actualization and self esteem needs into a Growth category and suggested that when higher order needs are not met, people will invest more time and energy in lower order needs. There are several variations of these motivational theories but they all indicate that human beings have the need to expand the human mind and explore their interconnectedness and the concept of a universal mind.

The first research laboratories to study the human psyche were the ancient caves and ashrams of India and Tibet. The dynamics of an individual soul (**jivatma**) and a universal soul (**paramatma**) were studied from different angles and the journey of self realization was thoroughly explored. Many principles were advocated and they created the stepping stones for various spiritual paths and traditions in the Eastern and Western worlds. In essence, we inherited a wonderful toolbox for our individual spiritual pursuit. The day we were born, the poet Rumi tells us, a ladder was set up for us to reach heaven – we must start climbing.

As we navigate the path of self discovery, several obstacles surface. From early childhood, we learn to cling to someone or something – parents, spouses and children and later to money, status and title. This seems to define our nature. Some spiritual paths advocate total detachment and moving away from these crutches. Others, like the bhakti path, advise us to take advantage of the tendency to be attached to things and make use of the same technique to connect with the Divine Energy. This is the approach of doing everything with noble intent and surrendering the fruits of our efforts to the Divine.

The Bhagavad Gita (song of the Lord), is the oldest textbook on philosophy and psychology. It is an ancient Sanskrit Granth taken from Canto 6, Chapters 25-42 of the *Mahabharata* and consists of 700 verses in 18 Chapters. It is commonly referred to as the *Gita* or *Gitopanishad*. The *Mahabharata* itself is a huge Sanskrit epic that contains interesting personality stories and chronicles the great war between the Pandavas and Kauravas, which some historians have placed around 3139 BC. The Kurukshetre War took place towards the end of Dwapara Yuga as the world was descending into the current Kali Yuga, or Dark Age.

In this important book of *Gita*, we are introduced to the Divine Energy as Lord Krishna who plays the role of a charioteer. He guides the chariot as Arjuna, after some initial reluctance, pursues his obligations along the path of life. The Sanskrit word for a chariot is "**ratha**" from which is derived the Latin word "rota" and also the English derivative "roto" for a wheel or spinning. As the wheels spin and take the chariot along the path, in a like fashion we also spin and navigate our human body on Earth. The teachings in *Gita* have inspired generations of people from various cultures and religions. It also created the foundation for the development and practice of Yoga and Ayurveda as universal healing modalities. The cumulative wisdom of the *Gita* is precious and timeless.

This book will select one verse from each of the eighteen Chapters of *Bhagavad Gita* and discuss the lessons that we can learn from these powerful words of wisdom. It will also provide a spectrum of ideas and suggestions that can be used in contemporary societies to remain grounded, centered and balanced in our daily activities. In the House of Krishna there is work for us to do, but the spiritual rewards are significant. Included in each Chapter are some discussion questions to encourage dialogue and appreciation of different ideas, opinions and perspectives on spiritual development. There are also some inspirational quotes at the end of each Chapter to help consolidate the messages.

The discussions in this book will provide a good foundation to yoga students and Yoga Teachers in their study of Yoga Philosophy. It will also be of interest to devotees in various Hindu Mandirs, and it can be used in lectures and discussions at various Satsangs internationally. As life changes and we continue to evolve spiritually, my hope is that you will find some guidance and advice in the following Chapters.

Hari Om Shanti

Namaste.
The Divinity within me salutes the Divinity within you.

ONE

The Playing Field

BHAGAVAD GITA
CHAPTER 1, VERSE 1

Dhrtarastra uvaca
Dharma ksetre kuru ksetre
Samaveta yuyutsavah
Mamakah pandavas chaiva
Kim akurvata Sanjaya

TRANSLATION

Dhrtarastra uvaca	King Dhrtarastra said
dharma kshetre	a place of pilgrimage
Kurukshetre	the field of material action
samaveta	assembled
yuyutsava	with a desire to fight
mamakah	my sons
Pandavah	the sons of Pandu
chaiva	and certainly
kim	what
akurvata	did they do
Sanjaya	Sanjaya

MEANING

King Dhrtarastra asks his assistant Sanjaya:
"When my sons and the sons of Pandu assembled on the holy field at Kurukshetre with the desire to fight, what transpired?"

The Playing Field 3

SIGNIFICANCE AND LESSONS

As a teenager growing up in Guyana, South America, I often wondered why a great religious book like *The Bhagavad Gita* would start with a discussion of wars and battles and fighting, when the message of Peace and Love seemed to be the desired objective. I once asked my Dad about this, and he said it had a deeper meaning than just what appeared on the surface. After 50 years of fights with various work associates in corporate boardrooms, battles with colleagues in academic circles, and disagreements with family members, I am beginning to get the message! It's about the internal battles within each of us.

Every night we go to sleep, a movie is playing. Every morning we wake up, we are faced with a decision. Which direction do I take? In the Cherokee tradition, the elders tell an interesting story. In each human being, they say, there is a good wolf and a bad wolf. Every day these two wolves are fighting inside of us. The elders will often ask you the important question. Which wolf will win? After a pause, they will ask the question again, and give the answer. Which wolf will win? The wolf that you feed.

In the first verse of the first Chapter of *Gita*, we are given an insight into the playing field on which life unfolds. This is referred to as Dharmashetre and Kurukshetre – a field of material action and also a holy field. This field of action is the human body with its physical, mental and spiritual components forming a network on which all of life's activities take place. We've often heard that the body is a temple and we should treat it as such. This human body is certainly a holy field, a gift given to us after many incarnations. In the *Ramayana*, another great Hindu epic, we are told:

Bare bhaaga, manusha tanu paava
Sura durlabha saba, granthanhi gaavaa
Saadhana dhaama, moksha kara dwaara
Paai na jehi, paraloka sanwaara

It is through great good fortune that you have secured a human body. It is suitable for spiritual endeavours and it is a gateway to liberation.

The enquiry into the activities on the battlefield (human body) is made by the mind, which is symbolically portrayed to us as the blind King Dhritarashtra. The name Dhrtarastra can be traced to the Sanskrit words, dhritam rastram yena, which means 'one who rules by tightly holding the reins'. The human mind is regal and powerful in stature, hence the reference to a King. The human mind is also blind, in the sense that it is merely a blank canvas on which the five senses can write and create impressions. In this context, the blind King is seeking an objective report from Sanjaya. The name Sanjaya means 'victorious', indicating one who is self-realized, impartial and one who can provide an unbiased and impartial opinion on which important decisions can be made.

Since *Gita* deals with the teachings of metaphysical science, it is significant that this sacred dialogue took place on a battlefield at Kurukshetre and not in a temple, ashram or in a secluded forest. Here, in the middle of noise and the hustle bustle of chariots, elephants, horses, armour and weapons, Krishna chooses to impart his universal advice to Arjuna. This is an outdoor katha (story) at its best. This is the playing field of life, amidst the noise and haste. In Max Ehrmann's

1927 poem *Desiderata*, we are advised to go placidly amidst the noise and haste of this world. "You are a child of the universe," he reminds us.

HORSES AND CHARIOT

The Bhagavat Gita provides its readers with a majestic and visually profound analogy of a human being. Paramahansa Yogananda describes this quite well in his book Bhagavat Gita – God Talks With Arjuna. The human body is the chariot, the soul is the owner of the chariot, intelligence is the charioteer, and the senses are the horses. This is shown in Figure 1 on Page 16. The reins of a chariot receive and relay the impulses from the horses and the guidance of the charioteer. The mind provides some coordination to the five senses just as the reins keep together the several horses pulling the chariot.

The timeless message of *Gita* not only refers to one historical battle but also extends to the constant conflict between the forces of good and evil, at an individual level and at a social level. Each person has to fight his/her own battle of Kurukshetra. It is important for us all to be aware that there is a constant warfare in our kingdom. It's a battle between spirit and matter, health and disease, self-control and temptation. The key is a sense of awareness that we all have some good qualities and some undesirable characteristics. There is a sinner in every saint and a saint in every sinner. It is the constant struggle between these two diametrically opposed camps that creates our biggest challenge in life.

THE AGENDA

In the very first verse of *Gita*, we are told that the Pandavas (representing the positive forces) are positioning themselves to do battle with the Kauravas (the negative forces). They are equally competent in their capabilities, and hence the word 'samaveta' is used, indicating that they are of the same strength. Their agenda is also clear. They are not there to support each other. They exist as opposing entities, and the word yuyutsava indicates that they have assembled at Kurukshetre with the specific intention of fighting each other. Symbolically, the kingdom of body and mind rightfully belongs to the Soul. As the Soul asserts itself to defend its territory by adopting noble thoughts, words and actions, the armies of the Ego rise up to prevent this with a matrix of temptations and vices. From a historical perspective, as outlined in the Mahabharat, the good virtues (Pandavas) reigned in the Kingdom until Duryodhana, the son of the blind King Dhritarashtra took away their kingdom. So what we are seeing is an attempt by the "good guys" to reclaim the throne from the "bad guys". It should be no surprise that the plot of most movies, plays and stories fit into this general theme. It's art mimicking life.

The concept of a battlefield is not confined, by any means, to Eastern philosophical thinking. You will find reference to it in other cultures and religions. I am a fan of Bluegrass music and Southern Baptist spiritual hymns. In the early part of 2010, I spent some time teaching Yoga in the states of Kentucky and Tennessee in USA. There is popular hymn that is sung with deep devotion in the churches and at Bluegrass festivals around these states:

> I'm on the battlefield for my Lord
> The battle is almost done
> I'll serve Him until I'm gone

Yes, I'm on the battlefield for my Lord

When I heard this hymn for the first time, I asked an older parishioner about it and she said it has been sung for generations in the cotton plantations in southern United States. I asked what it meant, and she replied that it is a reminder that life is very much like a battlefield.

From the time we are born, the struggle starts. As an infant, we are torn between instinctively seeking comfort and survival and the relative helplessness of the underdeveloped body instrument. A child is divided between the desire to play and the need to study and learn. Teenagers and young adults are confronted with a variety of concerns that they may be unprepared to address. Peer pressures, temptations of sex, greed and rebellion are all forces that pull our young people away from honing positive life skills and completing their formal education. Adults are constantly tossed between righteous living habits and destructive behaviours, disease and unhappiness.

THE FIGHT OF FIGHTS

This external and internal battle plays out throughout life. In the history of boxing, one of the greatest fights we have witnessed is the 1975 fight between Mohammed Ali and Joe Frazier in Manilla, Philippines, nicknamed the "Thrilla in Manilla". This took place during the flamboyant reign of Ferdinand and Imelda Marcos in the Phillipines, who seized the opportunity to showcase their country to the world. Each side had its own army of trainers, advisers, corner men, media personnel, physiotherapists and supporters. It was quite an international event.

We recall that these two boxers had been close friends. Frazier had helped Ali with support, funding and advice when he was disbarred from fighting due to his refusal to join the US Army and fight in the Vietnam War. Before the fight, Ali taunted Joe about his ugliness, clumsiness, and blackness, priding himself as a converted Muslim and a progressive black man in the Nation of Islam. He crossed the line in his public taunts and insults of Joe as a Tomboy and a traitor to the black people of America, something that deeply wounded Joe and emotionally scarred him. Naturally, the press and the people with financial interests in boxing pounced on this and amplified the opinions and intentions. The fight was stopped before the start of the fifteenth round because it was deemed too dangerous. Unfortunately, this experience created a bitter feud between these two great fighters.

This was a case of ego, money and fame being played out on an international stage with large financial stakes. The horses (senses) were running frantically in all directions in pursuit of material objectives and rational thinking seemed to be nowhere in sight. It was as if there was no charioteer to guide the galloping horses. These deep internal conflicts clouded their judgement for years to come and they have oscillated between public apologies and insults ever since. While the world was entertained with the glamour of the external fight, there was a fierce internal battle within each boxer which eventually shaped their later lives.

Both Mohammed Ali and Joe Frazier have held the prestigious title of heavyweight champion of the world. Who won the fight? Today Frazier is in his early sixties, living modestly and teaching in a deprived neighbourhood in Philadelphia. He lost most of his fortune acquired from boxing and is struggling with health issues. Ali is in his late sixties and has done well financially. He was diagnosed with Parkinson's disease in 1984 and gets around with assistance. The strange irony is that we expend so much of our health to acquire wealth, and then spend much of our wealth to regain our health.

THE BACKDROP

The first chapter of *Gita* creates the backdrop from which the advice of Krishna is given. Many of the initial verses describe the strength of each army and the military skills the warriors bring to the battleground. Great detail is taken to outline these diverse skills of the fighters in order that we can get a good appreciation for the importance of each of our emotions and behaviours - good and bad. Our ego is sometimes referred to as the pseudo soul and its warriors are greed, anger, lust and all the emotions that accompany material desires. Their halls of residence are the lumbar, sacral and coccygeal centres, or the three lower chakras. The positive and noble soldiers of love, compassion and forgiveness reside in the medulla, cervical and dorsal centres of our body, or the three upper chakras. The divine spark of jiva atma, or the individual soul, enters and resides in the medulla oblongata.

The notion that we all have an army of divine qualities has been expressed in different cultures. Swami Vivekanand tells us that we are all spiritual beings having a material existence at this time. In 1 Corinthians 3.16 of the *Holy Bible*, Jesus reminds us:

> Know ye not that ye are the Temple of God
> And the Spirit of God dwelleth in you?

The Buddhist approach is to get in touch with the divine qualities that are already inside each person. After all, we are eternal beings on a cosmic journey. Lama Yeshe cautions us against too much supermarket information crowding our minds and suppressing the noble qualities within us. Ultimately it is a daily battle between the Pandavas and the Kauravas, the forces of good and bad. Recognizing this and empowering the soldiers of positive actions seem to be the cardinal message of Krishna. There is some wonderful advice in Sanskrit:

Durjanam prathamam vande
Sajjanam tadanantaram

It means that we should worship the bad person and then worship the good person. The bad person is slipping and giving us an example of how not to behave and the good person is providing an ample role model for us to follow. The advice is to recognize the different roles and responsibly and embrace both sides of our personality – it is the yin and yang of life.

DISCUSSION QUESTIONS

1. What makes a battlefield the ideal backdrop for the delivery of Krishna's message?
2. Why did King Dhrtarastra need an objective report of the opposing armies from Sanjaya?
3. Is the public perception of wars and battles different today from the time when the Bhagavad Gita was written?
4. What places and events could you use today to discuss the wisdom of Krishna?

INSPIRATIONAL QUOTES

There is no key to happiness.
The door is always open.
— *Unknown*

The line separating good and evil,
passes neither between states nor between classes,
but through the middle of each human heart.
— *Aleksandr Solzhenitsyn*

All of us, the great and the little, have need of each other.
— *Aesop*

Don't depend on the body,
It is only a cage.
It will be left behind and the bird will be gone.
Before that happens, take care of the bird.
— *Osho*

Ever since happiness heard your name,
it has been running through the streets
trying to find you.
— *Hafiz*

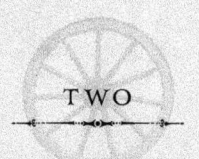

TWO

Power of the Senses

BHAGAVAD GITA
CHAPTER 2, VERSE 67

Indriyanam hi charatam
Yan mano 'nuvidhiyate
Tad asya harati prajnam
Vayur navam ivambhasi

TRANSLATION

indriyanam	of the senses	*tat*	that
ambhasi	on the water	*asya*	his
hi	certainly	*harati*	takes away
charatam	while roaming	*prajnam*	intelligence
yat	with which	*vayuh*	wind
manah	the mind	*navam*	boat
anuvidhiyate	constantly engaged	*iva*	like

MEANING

Just as a boat on the water is swept away by a strong wind, even one of the roaming senses on which the mind focuses can carry away a person's intelligence.

NATURE AND THE SENSES

Our senses of touch, sight, smell, taste and sound are the physiological capacities that provide inputs for our perception. Each one of our senses is a faculty by which external or internal stimuli are conveyed to the brain centers where they are registered as sensations. They are our antenna to the external environment in which we live. The senses are essentially instruments of the mind. The simile employed by the above verse is an important one. It is intended to illustrate the powerful nature of the senses and imply the need for awareness, monitoring and the prudent management of our senses.

Discussions about the five senses (**panchanam indriyanam**) are found in different writings throughout history. The earliest allegorical

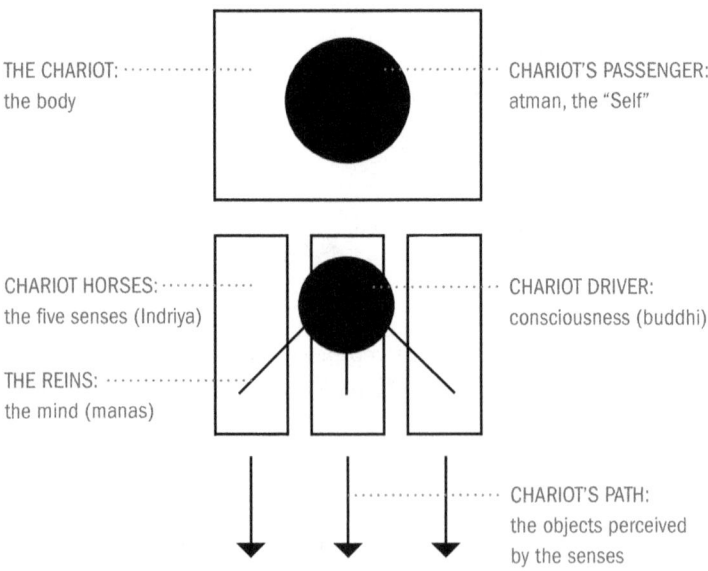

FIGURE 1: The Body Chariot

representation was in the Katha Upanishad (approximately 6th century BC) outlined as five horses drawing the chariot of the body and guided by the mind as the chariot proceeds along its path (Figure 1). Such visual depictions became popular with early painters, poets, sculptors and musicians in expressing their creative ideas. In the 1671 masterpiece oil-on-canvas work of the Dutch painter Gerard de Lairesse, *Allegory of the Five Senses*, each of the figures allude to one of the senses. This is shown in Figure 2 (below). Sight is the reclining boy with a convex mirror. Hearing is the cupid-like boy with a triangle. Smell is represented by the girl with flowers. Taste is the woman with the fruit. Touch is depicted by the woman holding the bird.

FIGURE 2: Gerard Lairesse - Allegory of the Five Senses (1671)

STAYING ON COURSE

In this *Gita* verse, the **buddhi** or faculty of intelligence is likened to a boat which can be tossed around by the wind or any of the senses.

A strong wind could prevent a boat from reaching its destination in two ways. It could throw the boat off course by forcibly pushing it into another direction or it could capsize and sink the ship. However, a skilled captain could manipulate the sails or engine to make the wind favourable so that the boat can be kept on course. In addition, the force of the wind itself could expedite the journey and cause the boat to reach its destination faster. It becomes an issue of how we utilize the five senses given to us. It seems so odd to me that this subject matter is something that is not generally taught in schools, colleges and universities. As a society, we make the assumption that people will somehow pick up this knowledge along life's path and figure this out from their own experiences.

As I'm writing this chapter on September 2nd, 2010, there is some "Breaking News" on Canadian television stations. There always seems to be breaking news on television! A Canadian Family Court Judge in Manitoba has stepped down from the bench today in reaction to allegations of having nude pictures of herself on an online pornographic website and, along with her lawyer husband, attempting to coerce a former client of her husband to sleep with her. This sent shock waves through the legal community in Canada. This is mentioned here not to judge any of the allegations or parties involved, but simply to illustrate the power of our senses and the type of trouble we can get into due to indiscretions and lapses in judgment. When the mind yields its steering to the raging storm of the senses, a person's self control needs to be strong. Regardless of our education, wealth or status in society, any one of our roaming senses can temporarily cloud our intelligence and create havoc in our lives.

From a practical perspective, the driver of life's chariot is not advised to kill his sense horses out of fear that they would run around wildly. That would be unwise. It is advisable, and indeed necessary, to harness the horses so that they could perform in compliance with the instructions of the driver. It is in this context that Jesus gave the following advice in the *Bible, Matthew 18.8*:

> "Wherefore if thy hand or foot offend thee, cut it off, and cast them from thee. It is better for thee to enter into life halt or maimed, rather than having two hands or two feet to be cast into everlasting fire."

In no way is this recommending literal dismemberment of body parts but rather the severance of the impulses that encourage them to get into trouble. The removal of a man's eyes does not eliminate his desire for sensual pictures or videos. What is required is the removal of the desire or the appetite for such objects. The story is told of a compulsive thief who, in repentance, cut off both his hands, but so compulsive was his habit that he soon started to steal things with his mouth and toes!

MANAGEMENT OF THE SENSES

One of the more challenging tasks facing human beings is the prudent management of our senses. One develops a liking for harmful sensual pleasures by thinking about these sense pleasures. Much of our modern advertisements and marketing campaigns use the lure of the human senses in creating a demand for products and services. It is no wonder that three of the largest industries today are tobacco, alcohol and pharmaceutical products. The desire for sense pleasures comes from thinking about sense pleasures. Anger comes when a desire is not fulfilled, and greed for more pleasure comes after that desire is fulfilled. A person is at peace when desires enter the mind without creating a disturbance, just as the waters from various rivers enter the ocean without creating a disturbance.

One of the strategies used in managing our senses is to constantly engage them in the natural environment. Be an outdoors person. Breathe fresh air – go for walks, jog, ski, etc. Smell beautiful flowers in gardens and parks. See beautiful natural settings in mountains, rivers and trails. Touch trees, rocks and waterfalls. The psychology of this approach is that the mind tends to connect more easily with universal Energy as we bond with the five great elements (**panch maha bhutas**) of earth, water, air, fire and space. I have a friend in Ireland who says its so much better to admire God's creation than sit in a church and admire ours!

In the world of Yoga, the sage Patanjali outlined an eight limbed approach called Ashtanga Yoga. The fifth stage is named **Pratyahara** or withdrawal of the senses. Here the discussion focuses on the restraint of the senses and the Yogi takes action to guard the doors of the five senses, thereby monitoring the activities that enter into the human mind. In his *Yoga Sutras, Samadipada*, Chapter 1.2, Patanjali writes:
Yogash chitta vrittri nirodha (Yoga is the restraint of the fluctuations in the activities of the mind field).

The focus here is on watching, monitoring and restraining any undesirable thoughts as they enter the field of the human mind. At the start of most yoga classes, we ask participants to take a few minutes and center themselves, bringing awareness and attention to the simple act of breathing. Breathing is the only function of the automatic nervous system that you can influence. It is interesting to note that, in our contemporary world, most of us pay attention to what we eat and drink, but few of us really pay attention to the toxic information that is beamed to us on television, computer screens, cell phones, iPod, iPad, etc. The level of violence, rudeness and sarcasm in images, conversations, e-mails and text messages is simply appalling. This represents an area of electronic information that we should all monitor and selectively consume.

Some writers describe the senses as ice and the mind as the water. Essentially they are seen as the same H2O existing in different states. The five senses can also be likened to five arms of an octopus. They are out there. They receive and bring stimulus from outside to our mind. The question is what does our mind do with the information brought in by the senses. How is the information processed? What do we utilize and what do we discard? We all want to be happy, no one wants to be sad. The interesting thing about the human mind is that it cannot hold emotions of happiness or sadness. When we are happy, we radiate and we tell everyone. We text message and e-mail friends, we phone people, we talk and we simply beam with joy. When we are sad, the world hears about it. We complain about our plight, who did us wrong, when, and what we are going to do about it. Much of the personal text messages and telephone calls we make communicate these emotions to family, friends and colleagues around the world.

When we recognize the power of our five senses, we can engage them to work in our favour. Most of us pray for long life (**ayur**), health (**arogya**) and happiness (**saukhyam**). With this intent and for religious, social, spiritual and other reasons, we attend temples, churches, mandirs, mosques, gurudwaras, synagogues etc. Here is how the five senses are utilized in this process:

Darshan (see) – Seeing the Lord, a symbol or representation thereof.
Shravan (hear) – Hear the praises of the Lord in sermons, hymns, chants, kirtans, bhajans etc.
Sparsha (touch) – Touch the image, a symbol or representation
Gandha (smell) – Smell flowers, incense, fruits etc.
Rasana (taste) – Taste wine, biscuit, fruits, prashad

It is in this context that we are advised to engage and utilize the five senses in the pursuit of noble intent and honourable objectives. With this template in mind, we gradually come to recognize that we are multisensory beings on a remarkable journey in life. This invites a shift in our perspective. It means doing our work to the best of our ability and leaving the fruits of our actions to the Divine will. Seeing the big picture in this respect helps us to maintain this perspective.

> When the five senses and the mind are stilled,
> When the intellect is motionless,
> That, they say, is the Highest Way.
> – *Maitri Upanishad*

> **DISCUSSION QUESTIONS**
> 1. What strategies could you use to monitor the activities of the five senses?
> 2. Which of the five senses (seeing, hearing, smelling, tasting and touching) are easier to manage? Why?
> 3. How difficult is it to manage our thoughts today in a world of rapid multi-tasking, innovative advertising, and advances in information technology?

INSPIRATIONAL QUOTES

Habit is the sixth sense that overrules the other five.
– *Arabic Proverb*

The senses do not deceive us, but the judgment does
– *Van Goethe*

Love is of all passions the strongest,
for it attacks simultaneously the head, the heart and the senses.
– *Lao Tsu*

मनजदेहमिमं यावि दर्लभं कामाधगम्य स्वैरैरपि वांजतमू
विषयनंपटामपहाय वै भजत रे मनुजाः कमलापतिमू ॥
(शंकराचार्य)

You have been blessed with a human birth, which is difficult
to attain. Don't waste the precious moments of your life
in pursuit of sensual pleasures.
– *Shankaracharya*

THREE

Non-Attachment to the
Fruits of Action

BHAGAVAD GITA
CHAPTER 3, VERSE 19

Tasmad asaktah satatam
Karyam karma samachara
Asakto hy acharan karma
Param apnoti purusah

TRANSLATION

tasmad	therefore	*hi*	certainly
asaktah	without attachment	*acharan*	performing
satatam	constantly	*karma*	work
karyam	as duty	*param*	supreme
karma	at work	*apnoti*	achieves
samachara	perform	*purusah*	a man
asakto	unattached		

MEANING

Therefore, without attachment to the fruits of activities, one should constantly perform material and spiritual actions. By doing actions without attachment, one attains supreme heights.

SIGNIFICANCE

This verse captures the essence of Krishna's message in the *Gita*. It is one of those verses that Shakespeare would say needs to be chewed and digested, for it succinctly captures the approach that we should adopt in life. The operative Sanskrit word here is **asaktah** which means 'without attachment'. We often hear that money is the root of all evil. My take on this is simple - it is the attachment to the things that money can buy that is the root of all evil. It is the lure of the house, cottage, car, status, power, title etc. that pulls us into, and keeps us attached to, the world of materiality. We are therefore advised to engage in material and spiritual actions, but remain unattached to whatever we have acquired as a result of these efforts. The challenge is how to do this in a world that places so much emphasis on our acquisitions and the quantum of material and intellectual success that we have accumulated.

The Wall Street Journal ran a recent article on the greed of CEO's in the United States of America. While their companies are struggling to stay in business, the lavish and obscene spending on parties and trivia seem to defy any shred of corporate responsibility. Despite amassing considerable personal wealth, these CEO's continued to spend like drunken sailors even after some of them were convicted. The article mentioned some research which identified various reasons for such behaviour. Five main factors were cited:

1. Comparing themselves with other CEO's
2. Keeping score with others
3. Sense of Entitlement
4. Delusions of Grandeur
5. Compensating for poor self-image.

The primary reason for this behaviour appears to be a strong attachment of the ego to the wealth already acquired, and the fear of losing that status and power. It seemed that the identity of the executive became wrapped up in the title, influence and possessions and it became increasingly difficult to detach from that identification.

The best advice I received in this context came from my mother. After I received my first pay cheque at age 18 working for a large British bank, I was enthusiastically telling her about what I can purchase and how much I can save before I reach age 21. With a look sculpted by years of hard work and experience in the rice fields of Guyana, she looked at me and said:

"You must learn to keep money in your pocket, not your head."

Every time I become engulfed in ego and pseudo achievements, I reflect on these potent words of wisdom. They have kept me in balance and on solid ground.

THE ART OF DETACHMENT

In 1975, a wonderful book entitled *A Course in Miracles* was published by the Foundation for Inner Peace in California, USA. It was the joint effort of two people - Helen Schucman and William Thetford, Professors of Medical Psychology at the College of Physicians and Surgeons at Columbia University in New York City. They were anything but spiritual, and their relationship with each other was often strained and difficult. The Head of the Academic Department announced that he was tired of all the angry and aggressive attitudes and figured that there must be another way to conduct university business. Out of this search came *The Course - a Text, a Workbook for Students and a Manual for Teachers*. Although Christian in its statement, *The Course* deals with universal spiritual themes, emphasizing one version of the curriculum.

In Lesson 128 of the *Course in Miracles*, the authors explained the need for non-attachment to materiality as discussed in the *Bhagavad Gita*. They suggested the following affirmation:

> The world I see holds nothing that I want.
> The world you see holds nothing that you need to offer you.
> Each thing you value here is but a chain that binds you to the world. Let nothing that relates to body thoughts delay your progress to salvation.
> Protect your mind throughout the day as well. And when you think you see some value in an aspect or an image of the world, refuse to lay this chain upon your mind, but tell yourself with quiet certainty:
> This will not tempt me to delay myself.
> The world I see holds nothing that I want.

In many ways this modern affirmation echoes the wisdom contained in the *Mahamritunjaya Mantra* which has recited for centuries by yogis, swamis and devotees of Lord Shiva.

> *Om Triyambakam Yajamahe*
> *Sugandhim pushti vardanam*
> *Urva arukam eva bandanat*
> *Mrityor moksheyama amritaat*

> We pray to Lord Shiva.
> As a cucumber is separated from the vine when it is ripe,
> May He liberate us from death to achieve immortality.

MAINTAINING PROPER PERSPECTIVE

As a result of our education, beliefs and social conditioning, we make certain assumptions about the relationship between our physical, mental and spiritual bodies. Swami Chinmayananda, in one of his more humorous lectures, clarifies the location of the human mind. He asked "If I put your head near to the fireplace, your feet into a bucket of cold water, and I tickle your tummy, can you tell me - where is your mind?" Somehow we think of the human mind as an organ or entity somewhere inside our body. In reality, it's the other way around. The human body is inside the human mind. Maybe it will help if we can see the mind as a field of energy and information that is inside our body and also extends outside and around our body. It constantly receives information and communicates information.

DISCUSSION QUESTIONS

1. Why is it easy to be swayed by material acquisitions in the modern world?
2. Is money the major motivator in our society?
3. If you had the wealth to pay off all your debts and have a regular monthly source of income, what work would you do?

INSPIRATIONAL QUOTES

Bondage is of the mind.
Freedom too is of the mind.
— *Ramakrishna*

Be in the world, but not of it.
— *Jesus*

Some of us think holding on makes us strong,
but sometimes, it is letting go.
— *Herman Hesse*

The cause of all unhappiness and misery in this world
is our attachment to name and form.
— *Gururaj Ananda Yogi*

Being totally busy is a wasteful way of living.
— *Zen saying*

Time will generally lessen the interest of every attachment
not within the daily circle.
— *Jane Austen*

FOUR

Divine Manifestations

BHAGAVAD GITA
CHAPTER 4, VERSE 7

Yada yada hi dharmasya
Glanir bhavati Bharata
Abhyutthanam adharmasya
Tadatmanam srjamy aham

TRANSLATION

yada yada	whenever and wherever
hi	certainly
dharmasya	virtue, religious practices
glanih	decline
bhavati	manifest, come forth
bharata	descendant of Bharata
adhyutthanam	rise, predominance
adharmasya	evil, unrighteousness
tada	at that time
atmanam	self
srjami	manifest
aham	I

MEANING

Whenever and wherever there is a decline in virtuous actions and an increase in unrighteousness, I will manifest.

Divine Manifestations

ROLE OF AVATARS

The concept of omnipresence means that the Divine Source has the ability to manifest on Earth at any place, at any time and in any shape or form. This is generally referred to as an incarnation of God or an Avatar. It is important to note that it is not a human being that is born but the Energy of Divinity that is focused in this world of human beings. While it has the physical features of a human being to allow for interaction with people on Earth, it has the power, the grace and the blessing of God.

Swami Krishnananda from the Sivananda Ashram in Rishikesh notes in his 1994 article *The Coming of God on Earth*, that what incarnates is not a localized entity, an extra cosmic someone reigning far away from the kingdom of world, but it is the coming into formation of that which is Omnipresent. In Sanskrit, we refer to this as **virat swarupa** – the Supreme, Almighty form of God. Swamiji asks the question - "How many rays does the Sun have?" Whether we think it is one ray or several rays merging into one bright ray, this does not change the magnificence of the Sun.

One of the great consolations is knowing that the Divine Source has a keen interest in our well-being, and visits us at important times in our lives to assist us through difficult times. As I am writing this Chapter on October 12th, 2010, the amazing rescue of 33 Chilean miners is being televised live across the world. They were trapped some 2000 feet below ground for 69 days when the San Jose mine in Chile collapsed. The survival and rescue was history in the making. Nothing like this was ever done before. As the first miner came up in the Phoenix capsule, one member of the reporting team remarked that sometimes God gives us a cosmic tap on the shoulder to remind us of what great things are possible when we can pull together as a human race. This was a remarkable collective effort involving many people from different countries, and it was nothing short of a miracle.

Avatars come to Earth for three principal reasons. Firstly, they come to restore a sense of peace, harmony and confidence when the state of affairs has regressed into a situation of intolerable harmful behaviours. This may involve the removal of some institutions or individuals and the restoration of faith. We have seen this happen several times throughout human history. Secondly, they come to earth to act as role models so that we can emulate some of their behaviours, especially in interacting with others. Thirdly, avatars come here to teach. They travel in the region they are born and disseminate the messages of love, kindness and compassion. In this manner they make an impact and leave a lasting impression in the minds and hearts of human beings.

The presence of Divinity on Earth, time and time again, is to facilitate our return to the natural order of things - a state of peace, tranquility and harmony. The journey in life is not so much in exploring new frontiers as seeing the existing ones with new lenses. At some point in this journey, we begin to realize that this whole universe vibrates with one loving intention. In her book entitled *The Age of Miracles*, Marianne Williamson notes that when you align your intention with God's, you set in motion a kind of wind at your back. Things just seem to flow well.

DIVINE GUARANTEE

Moulana Jalalludin Rumi, the 13th century Sufi Poet, tells the following story:

> The lovely moon shone last night.
> She came to my house.
> "Leave me now " I said "I'm busy. I can't see you tonight."
> As she left, I heard her say "How sad, you won't open your door, even when a treasure comes."

It is interesting to observe how many times we are unable to recognize, acknowledge and benefit from the Divine Grace that is around us all the time. We get caught up in rushing around in a culture of material acquisition or pursuing skills designed only to enhance wealth accumulation. Many of us are so busy doing mundane things with such a frantic pace, racing up the ladder without much concern for where it is taking us. Most of us start out to be brilliant scientists, not philosophers, but end up being both. It is for this reason that the Divine Spirit takes on a human form so that we can see, touch and interact with a real person. The intent is to change our internal dialogue and refocus our energies towards spiritual development.

Like every society, every individual goes through the necessary evolutionary stages of development. At each stage there are concerns, obstacles and challenges. Whenever greed, malice, atrocities and wars reach a certain threshold, the Supreme Energy manifests in the form of masters who, through many incarnations, have advanced along their own spiritual paths. They may appear as minor saints and sages or as fully liberated beings, according to their own degree of self-realization. This is a formal guarantee which we can take as a personal consolation in tough times. In the Shri Ramcharitmanas version of Ramayan, we recall that people had endured a lot of hardships through the persecutions and atrocities of the evil King Ravan. They prayed intensely to Brahma, and we are told about this promise in Balkand:

> *Kaha biranci haripada sumiru*
> *Dharani dharai mana dhira,*
> *Prabhu bhamjihi daruna bipati*
> *Janata jana ki pira.*

"Have patience on Earth," said Brahma,
"and fix your mind on God. The Lord knows the distress of people
and will put an end to cruel suffering."

Later on in the Chapter, more specifics and details are provided about this manifestation for additional reassurance of the saints and sages. In this case, the Supreme Energy took the form of four brothers – Ram, Lakshman, Bharat and Shatrughan.

> *Jani darapahu muni siddha suresa*
> *Tumhahim lagi dharihaun narabes.*
> *Amsanha sahita manuja avatara*
> *Lehaum dina karabamsa udar.*
> *Tinha kem grha avatarihaum jai*
> *Raghukulatilaka so chariu bhai*

Fear not, O saints and sages.
For your sake, I will assume human form
with all my Divinity in the glorious solar race.
In their house (Dasrath and Kausalya)
I will become incarnate as four brothers, their pride and joy.

THE NEED FOR INTERVENTION

Much of the above discussion begs the question about the need for God to intervene on Earth when we seem to have the resources here to manage quite well. There has been a lot of scientific and technological progress in the efficient production of goods and services to meet the needs of human beings on Earth. The concern is in the interaction with one another, how we behave individually or as a member of a group in our work and social activities.

Some students of Psychology and Criminology are still amazed today at the results of the notorious 1971 Stanford Prison Experiment conducted by Dr. Phillip Zimbardo in which he explored the question of why good people do bad things. In his book entitled *The Lucifer Effect*, he discussed the concept of the inner demon in all of us, and explained that good and evil are the yin and yang of life. At some points in our life, we seem to resort to behaviours that are contrary to our own values and moral principles. The influence of authority figures and group expectations feature prominently in these scenarios.

Whenever the levels of destructive behaviours reach a certain threshold in any part of the world, Divine Intervention becomes necessary. It is much like a group of children playing happily in a park until one of the kids becomes mean and starts to bully the others. Things get out of hand and a parent or a guardian needs to intervene. Likewise, the need to restore order and safety on Earth becomes evident and the Cosmic Director appears on stage in a human form. This can take the form of a full or partial manifestation, depending on the need and the circumstances. It can be one full manifestation, as it was in the case of Lord Krishna. It can also be several people in a supportive role, as was the case with the four brothers in Ramayan who came collectively to address Ravan and his atrocities.

> **DISCUSSION QUESTIONS**
> 1. What is the most conspicuous feature or behavioural trait of a Divine Incarnation?
> 2. What unusual events generally precede the coming of an Avatar?
> 3. Do we witness partial manifestations of the Divine? What is their role in society?

INSPIRATIONAL QUOTES

Are you looking for me?
I am the breath inside the breath.
– *Kabir*

To find God,
You must welcome everything.
– *Rabindranath Tagore*

Because you cannot see Him,
God is everywhere.
– *Yasunari Kawabata*

God picks up his flute and blows,
and each note is a blessing coming through each of us.
– *Rumi*

So many gods, so many creeds,
So many paths that wind and wind,
While just the art of being kind
Is all the world really needs.
— *Ella Wilcox*

To the mind that is still, the whole universe surrenders.
— *Lao Tzu*

FIVE

The Inside Journey

BHAGAVAD GITA

CHAPTER 5, VERSE 24

Yo 'ntah-sukho 'ntar-aramas
Tathantar-jyotir eva yah
Sa yogi brahma-nirvanam
Brahma-bhuto 'dhigacchati

TRANSLATION

yah	who
antah-sukhah	happy from within
antah-aramah	enjoying from within
tatha	as well as
antah-jyotih	light within
eva	certainly
yah	anyone
sah	that
yogi	a mystic
Brahma-nirvanam	divine liberation
Brahma-bhutah	self realization
adhigacchati	attains

MEANING

One whose happiness is within, who is active and rejoices within, and whose focus is inward is actually the perfect Yogi. She/He is self realized, and ultimately attains Divine liberation.

THE JOURNEY WITHIN

This verse outlines the universal prescription for happiness. Organized religions approach this subject from the perspective of enlightenment and spiritual awakening, focusing on such outcomes as nirvana, moksha, satori and cosmic consciousness. People in eastern societies have been experimenting with this process for many centuries. Monks and yogis have travelled back and forth between the physical and spiritual realms in the caves and ashrams of India and Tibet. The process often uses various sensory deprivation techniques. Gradually, this cumulative knowledge permeated western societies and the richness and beauty of these mystical experiences began to fascinate and entice us.

There is a strong correlation between the process of going within oneself and that of transcending the physical plane. Mystics have taught us that you have to go deep within yourself in order to be free from the material attachments and associated emotions. Eastern philosophers claim that this responsibility is the single most important duty of human beings and is the main purpose of life on Earth. Unfortunately, many of us come to this realization quite late in life.

Sometimes the inward journey is imposed by various external circumstances and situations. After a devastating personal experience in 2002, it took me approximately four years of scattered searching to realize that until a wave dissolves into the ocean, it remains very limited in its abilities. I knew I had to go somewhere to heal, to change perspective and regain a sense of balance. I recalled the following words from a Rumi poem:

Change houses in your mind for a day.

It made sense. I knew what I had to do, but yet my heart was bleeding from many wounds, most of them self-imposed. My mind regressed to the words of an old bhajan (Hindu devotional song) that I had memorized early in life:

Gangaa me nahee, Jamunaa me nahee
Mahlo me nahee, Kutiyo me nahee
Jahaa, yaad karo Bhagwaan wahee
Oh, Jaha, yaad karo Bhagwaan yahi

God is not located in the Ganges river
nor in the Jamuna river,
Not in the palace,
Nor in the ashram.
Wherever Divinity is contemplated, that's where God is.

I realized that Divinity is everywhere, at all times, and in any place. The onus was definitely on me to invite Divinity to my heart, my mind and my whole being.

After a period of confusion and somewhat mixed introspection, I woke up one morning at 3 AM and wrote this personal promise to myself:

My Credo
I promise to honour my Soul
with Love, Kindness and Compassion.

> I now offer myself humbly as:
> A guardian of Nature
> A teacher of Health
> An ambassador of Peace
> – *The Author (Dec. 2006)*

The serenity, harmony and tranquility that subsequently followed served as a template to direct my teaching career, relationships and behaviours. To this day, it constitutes the framework from which my life unfolds.

DIFFERENT STROKES FOR DIFFERENT FOLKS

We are all made in the image of God, but we are all different personalities. Different ages, sexes, races, religions, education, professions and habits. One of the things I like in my home is a quilt. Here we have a beautiful, decorative and functional item that takes different pieces of cloth of different colours and textures, and arranges them so beautifully into the exquisite art of a warm bedspread, comforter or decoration for the home. Those of us living in the cold, northern climates of Canada will understand my appreciation for this on a cold winter night.

My intention in the above paragraph is to illustrate that we are all different human beings. Let us celebrate this quilt. Often I hear people say that I want to be with someone just like me. I don't think I'd like to be with someone who thinks, acts and behaves like me for too long. I have a hard enough time looking at myself in the mirror! We can celebrate our diversities and rejoice that we have common goals and aspirations. When we come down to brass tacks, we all want peace, love and happiness. This is where we engage our collective efforts.

I like music. I like listening to different music. I like watching live performances and listening to different people sing and play musical instruments. I also like playing music. We use music for entertainment and we also use music to connect to Divine Energy. Different people from different cultures use songs and chants in ceremonies and festivals. Sounds move from the ear to the soul. Tibetans live in high altitudes and use low pitched chants. The need to connect to Earth and root deeply in their faith is fundamental to the Buddhist philosophy. The Aboriginal cultures of North America who live in low plains use high pitched chants during round dances and other ceremonies. The need to reach upwards and connect to the Sky is central to their belief system that uses totem poles and the soaring eagle to symbolise the engagement of heavenly energies. While the vehicles may be different, we are all heading in the same direction along the journey of life.

THE BENEFITS

It is important to understand the benefits which can be gained from pursuing the inward journey of self discovery. It brings a sense of mental alertness and clarity. Powers of concentration increase and long term memory is enhanced. We can tap into an immense pool of inner strength and courage. People like Nelson Mandella, Mother Theresa and Mahatma Gandhi recognized this personal power. They accessed and utilized their inner potential to survive and triumph over intense physical and mental agony. As we reach inwards and tap into that eternal source of energy, our perceptions will sharpen and life will assume new dimensions. We will find endless possibilities unfolding before us with considerable ease and remarkable joy.

When Patanjali synthesized the science of yoga in his *Yoga Sutras*, he made specific reference to the eighteen "siddhis" or extraordinary abilities which are acquired by a human being as she/he progresses along the spiritual path. They come with the territory, so to speak. Those who advance far enough are able to prudently manage their emotions, regulate body temperature, read thoughts and assist in the healing of others. As these abilities gradually manifest, we should try to use them responsibly in the service of humanity. The challenge, as with other gifts, skills and talent, is to manage the concomitant rise of the ego.

The practice of centering oneself on a daily basis is one good way of starting this inward journey and maintaining a sense of peace, harmony and balance. Sitting quietly in a place away from noise and distractions physically removes us from the busy external environment. We can bring the focus to the act of breathing, inviting the breath into our body and then gently escorting it out. Gradually the mental chatter and noise of that busy train that runs inside of us starts to slow down. We can let the breath fuel and guide us to travel inward and align with the core of our being. We simply pull back and watch our thoughts as they surface and retreat – neither resisting nor encouraging any thought or emotion. This integration of body, mind and spirit creates a sense of interconnectedness with Supreme Energy. It opens our creative potential and taps into the inner pharmacy of our human system. Much like erasing and reloading data on a rewritable compact disc, this is a remarkably therapeutic way of starting or ending the day.

There is much wisdom in the following Biblical advice:

> If you bring forth what is inside you
> What you bring forth will save you.
> If you do not bring forth what is inside you
> What you do not bring forth will destroy you.
> – *The Gospel of St. Thomas*

DISCUSSION QUESTIONS

1. Why is it important to go within and be in harmony with yourself?
2. What is your biggest challenge in bringing your focus inward?
3. How could you assist someone in making the inward journey?

INSPIRATIONAL QUOTES

> Just when a caterpillar thinks life is over, it becomes a butterfly.
> – *Old Indian Proverb*

> There is a voice within that doesn't use words. Listen.
> – *Rumi*

> All the hemispheres in existence lie beside an equator in your heart.
> – *Hafiz*

> Man can live either on the circumference or at the centre.
> To live at the circumference is easy,

To live at the centre is a great challenge,
because you will be living there alone.
– *Osho*

All of us find our final peace in the innermost self.
– *Upanishads*

The great lesson is that the sacred is in the ordinary,
It is to be found in one's daily life,
in one's neighbours, friends and family,
in one's own backyard.
– *Abraham Maslow*

God has sent us out as his children,
and in that Divine role we must return.
– *Shri Yukteshwar*

SIX

The Practice of Yoga

BHAGAVAD GITA
CHAPTER 6, VERSE 17

Yuktahara viharasya
Yukta cestasya karmasu
Yukta svapna vabodhasya
Yugo bhavati dukha-ha

TRANSLATION

yukta	regulated
ahara	eating
viharasya	recreation
yukta	regulated
cestasya	engaged in social activities
karmasu	discharging work responsibilities
yukta	regulated
svapna-avabodhasya	sleep and wakefulness
yogo	practice of yoga
bhavati	becomes
dukha-ha	alleviating pain

MEANING

The practice of Yoga, which alleviates sorrow and discomfort, is accomplished by one who is regulated in the habits of eating, sleeping, recreation and work.

YOGA PHILOSOPHY

This verse captures the benefits of a consistent yoga practice by someone who follows a balanced lifestyle. It suggests the middle path as the vehicle for personal health management. Yoga comes from the Sanskrit word "yuj" which means to join, connect or link. It is the disconnection of individual consciousness from Supreme Collective Consciousness which creates most of the concerns we face in everyday life. The more we are disconnected, the more the Ego assets itself. As we create paths to connect with our Source, we see ourselves as part of the Divine mosaic. Yoga is the practice which joins individual consciousness to its Supreme Energy Source, creating a sense of divine blessedness as we disengage from the pleasures of the senses. It is the reason why we experience a somewhat buoyant feeling of pseudo-ecstasy after a yoga class.

Yoga practices are based on the laws of Nature. Nature is not specific to a particular religion, faith or philosophy. It is true that the science of Yoga was developed in India from the foundation of a traditional Hindu way of life. In so far as this is so, most yoga teachers have a background knowledge of the *Bhagavad Gita*, Patanjali's *Yoga Sutras*, *Hatha Yoga Pradipika* and other related textbooks. Some people in the West come to Yoga practice for health reasons, usually after disappointment with contemporary medical treatments. This is to be applauded. However, a practice of 1.5 hours once a week will probably not make a significant difference. Yoga is a way of life. It is more the consistency of the practice that matters, not the intensity.

An overview of yoga philosophy would consist of a discussion of the subtle energy of the human system, the koshas, nadis and chakras. It would also extend to a study of the three gunas and the ayurvedic concepts of dosha body types. The intention is to understand how we can use our breathing and musculoskeletal movements to connect with the mind and the universal source of energy. Yoga and Ayurveda gives us a wonderful healing modality to maintain a balanced and healthy lifestyle.

As a sidebar, most practitioners of Yoga have a liking for nature, first energy foods and the natural environment. In the western world, most yoga teachers are former fitness trainers, dancers, runners, cyclists, campers, canoeists and hikers. This important relationship with the earth, water, trees and rocks is what connects them to nature and to their authentic self. It also serves as a method to disconnect from a world of ego and illusion which can easily pull us into a downward spiral. The beauty of landscapes, the smell of vegetation and the sounds of birds are all wonders to behold in spring, summer, fall and winter. I have a friend who is a yoga teacher, runner, cyclist and hiker. I asked her about her passion for the outdoors one Sunday morning when people generally attend Church. She told me that she would rather admire God's masterpiece outside than sit in a church pew and admire ours. Needless to say, I went for a jog with her.

In contemporary societies, we generally see yoga as a physical discipline in which people twist themselves into a variety of poses, often assuming esoteric and exotic postures. While this is aesthetically pleasing and makes for great advertising, it is somewhat removed from the philosophy and intent of Yoga practice. As Yoga came out to the Western world, the glamour and appeal of the physical postures and practices assumed centre stage. People are generally attracted to what will make them look and feel better. In some ways, this approach has lifted Yoga to new heights of awareness and recognition in the western world, offering in the process many new products and services in the marketplace. Today Yoga is practiced in homes, studios, gyms, schools, community halls and workplaces. Yoga clothing is a hot fashion trend. It's cool, trendy and sexy. The East has come to the West, in style!

ESSENTIALS OF YOGA

Yoga is an ancient discipline that consists of **eight limbs** - referred to by Patanjali in the *Yoga Sutras* as ashtanga. The word **ashtanga** consists of two Sanskrit words - **ashta**, meaning eight and **anga**, meaning a part (or limb) of the body. In his book *The Heart of Yoga*, (compulsory reading for yoga teachers in training), T.K.V. Desikachar puts this approach in perspective. From conception through a child's full development, all limbs of the fetus grow simultaneously. The body does not sprout an arm first, then a leg, and so on. Similarly, on the path of yoga all eight aspects develop concurrently and in an interrelated way. Here is a brief outline of the *Eight Limbs of Yoga*:

1. Yamas

These are five social attitudes (sometimes called restraints) which guide our behaviours as we interact with others and live as a member of any community. The five behaviour patterns are:

- Ahimsa - non violence, kindness and consideration
- Satya - speaking the truth
- Asteya - not stealing or embezzling
- Brahmacharya - responsible behaviour in sensual activities
- Aparigraha - not taking unfair advantage of a situation

2. Niyamas

These are five personal behaviours or principles that we should adopt in our everyday life. They are:
- Sauch – cleanliness of body and mind
- Santosh – contentment and modesty
- Tapas – leading a disciplined life
- Swadhyaya – self inquiry and lifelong learning
- Ishwarapranidhana – surrendering to Supreme Consciousness

3. Asanas

Asana means a posture. It is derived from the Sanskrit root as which means to sit or to be established in a particular position. Asanas refer to the various physical postures used in yoga practice, eg: trikonasana – triangle posture, and adho mukha svanasana – downward facing dog posture.

4. Pranayama

Pranayama means to extend the life force (prana – vital energy, and ayama – to stretch or extend). It refers to the various breathing exercises which are done in yoga practices.

5. Pratyahara

Pratyahara is the practice of sensory withdrawal and turning your attention inwards. Essentially, it is listening to the body from the inside instead of taking in and reacting to stimuli from the external world.

6. Dharana

Dharana is intense concentration or focusing your attention on a single object such as a mantra, an image or the breath. The objective is to quiet the mental chatter that goes on in our heads and minds.

7. Dhyana

Dhyana is meditation, a state of alert stillness. Here you have stopped seeing things as separate objects and you see things in an interconnected, interrelated way.

8. Samadhi

Samadhi is the objective of our yoga practice. It is the ultimate connection with Universal Consciousness, representing a state of universal oneness. This is usually accompanied by a sense of effortless flow, bliss and complete well-being.

YOUR PERSONAL YOGA PRACTICE

It was Lao Tzu who reminded us that a journey of a thousand miles begins with a single step. This is also true in yoga. By definition, yoga consists of principles and practices designed to integrate and promote the health of the body and mind. There is no single solution or "miracle cure" for our pains and problems. However, regular yoga practice has been proven to assist in making us healthy, happy and peaceful. In her book *Dr. Yoga*, Nirmala Heriza notes that this is "where the rubber of the philosophy meets the road". Over the years of teaching yoga at a downtown studio in the city of Edmonton, I have observed the inner conviction and transformation of students through frequent, infrequent and occasional practice sessions. Once you have reached into your authentic self through a yoga practice, your inner wisdom has carved an inward path on which you can walk in times of joy and despair.

My preference is for a daily practice of Hatha and Iyengar styles of yoga. You can choose any style that you like and develop your personal practice. There are benefits to all styles of yoga. The various asanas are designed to strengthen the immune and cardiovascular systems. Most people are busy with work, family and social obligations and understandably, are unable to devote an hour and a half each day to such a practice. My recommendation is to get in some micro-sessions during the morning, mid-day or evenings hours. These are transition points during the day and ideally suited to yoga practice and body-mind fortification. You can supplement this by attending a full weekend class at a Yoga Studio to benefit from the instruction of a certified yoga teacher.

The best health benefits seem to come from some of the simple yoga postures. Each day you should do the posture you like the most, and the one you like the least. Take your time. Sometimes the best lessons are learnt from our mistakes. The error of the past is the wisdom of the future. Allow your experiences on the mat to be your teacher. They will guide you well. The opposite of what we like invariably contains a lesson for us. The slow, easy introspective poses are the ones that allow you to project from the core to the periphery, engaging muscular energy and extending outward and upward. In your practice, bring space into your joints and expand your body from the inside out. Here are the best postures recommended for three micro-sessions during the day:

Morning
1. Alternate Nostril Breathing
2. Downward Facing Dog
3. Sun Salutation (three cycles)
4. Child's Pose

Midday
1. Triangle Pose
2. Reversed Triangle
3. Warrior 1 and 2
4. Tree Pose

Evening
1. Viparata Karani (feet up against a wall)
2. Shoulder Stand and Plough Pose
3. Lying Spinal Twist
4. Savasana

If life gets to be so hectic (and it usually does) that you cannot spare the time to do your exercise routine during the day, then at least try to do three cycles of the classical Surya Namaskar (Sun Salutation). Here is an illustration and brief description of the twelve postures involved in each cycle of Sun Salutation:

SUN SALUTATIONS

Surya Namaskar
  "**Surya**" means Sun and "**Namaskar**" means salutation or worship.

The Sun Salutation consists of a beautiful set of **asanas** or postures that massage, detoxify, and stimulate almost every organ of the human body and bring suppleness and flexibility to the spine. The Sun Salutation is a wonderful way to warm up and stretch at the same time.

A SHORT COMPREHENSIVE WORKOUT

Surya Namaskar is a panacea for those living a busy lifestyle in large cities and are very pressed for time. It is also an opportunity to breathe and exercise adequately. In just ten to twelve minutes, your body gets a comprehensive and systematic workout. It is an ancient and unique exercise routine that combines breathing and musculoskeletal movements. Sun Salutation makes the muscles strong, supple and flexible and it tones every part of the body.

BENEFITS OF SURYA NAMASKAR

The postures stretch the spine, hamstrings and backs of the legs. They also strengthen the legs, arms, back, and stomach muscles. The back is bent and straightened, and the abdomen is compressed and stretched. It loosens up the joints, flexes the muscles, massages internal organs, and also activates the different systems of the body. Please see the following two pages for the twelve postures. *See Index (page 193) for enlarged photos of each pose.*

Pranamasana (Prayer Pose) **EXHALE**

Hasta Uttanasana (Raised Arms Pose) **INHALE**

Hastapaadasana (Standing Forward Bending Pose) **EXHALE**

Ashwa Sanchalanasana (Equestrian Pose) **INHALE**

Dandasana (Four-Limbed Staff Pose) **EXHALE**

Ashtanga Namaskara (Salute with the Eight Limbs Pose) **HOLD**

Bhujangasana (Cobra Pose)
INHALE

Adho Mukha Svanasana
(Downward-Facing Dog) **EXHALE**

Ashwa Sanchalanasana
(Equestrian Pose; Lunge) **INHALE**

Uttanasana (Standing Forward
Bending Pose) **EXHALE**

Hasta Uttanasana (Raised Arms Pose)
INHALE

Pranamasana (Prayer Pose)
EXHALE

You can find these postures in any yoga book or on the Internet and watch the demonstrations on YouTube. However, it is important to get the instruction of a yoga teacher to encourage proper alignment, breathing and transitioning safely from one posture to the next. The greatest energy on Earth is present when the night turns to day, and hence the early morning hours are best suited to yoga practice. Try to maintain a regular morning practice before you start your day. Over time, you will notice the subtle changes in your posture, your breathing and your sleep. Remember that yoga is done on the edge, between comfort and pain. Listen to the intelligence of your body and go to your first edge. When your body opens up and invites you in deeper, accept the invitation, and proceed to the next edge. Yoga brings ancient wisdom to your body and your mind. It is the best gift that you can give to yourself.

DISCUSSION QUESTIONS

1. What are the major benefits that we can gain from practicing yoga?
2. How would you describe the functions of the nadis and the chakras?
3. Why has Yoga achieved such popularity in the western world?
4. Which is your favourite yoga posture? Which is the one you like the least?
5. Why is it important to maintain a consistent yoga practice?
6. What emotional changes do you notice in yourself after your yoga practice?

INSPIRATIONAL QUOTES

Consistent practice is the key to success in yoga.
— *Hatha Yoga Pradipika*

You will see the stars and the moon reflected in your Being.
— *Rumi*

Blessed are the flexible, for they shall not be bent out of shape.
— *Unknown*

Every blade of grass has its Angel that bends over it and whispers
"Grow, Grow."
— *The Talmud*

POETRY BY MIRABHAI

A GREAT YOGI

In my travels I spent time with a great yogi.
Once he said to me.
"Become so still you hear the blood flowing
through your veins."

One night as I sat quietly,
I seemed on the verge of entering a world inside so vast
I know it is the source of all of us.

SEVEN

Free Will
and Individual Choice

BHAGAVAD GITA

CHAPTER 7, VERSE 21

Yo yo yam yam tanum bhaktah
Sraddha yarcitum icchati
Tasya tasyacalam sraddham
Tam eva vidadhami aham

TRANSLATION

yo yo	whoever	*tasya tasya*	to him
yam yam	whichever	*acalam*	steady
tanum	form of divinity	*sraddham*	faith
bhaktah	devotee	*tam*	that
sraddhaya	with faith	*eva*	surely
arcitum	to worship	*vidadhami*	give
icchati	desires	*aham*	I

MEANING

Whatever form of Divinity a devotee desires to worship faithfully, I will surely strengthen her/his faith.

SYMBOLIC FORMS

This verse is an assurance that whatever mode of worship a person chooses in order to connect with Divinity, the Divine Consciousness will endorse this if the devotion is genuine. The use of the words "yo" and "yam" twice in this verse is purposely intended to illustrate the diversity of devotees on Earth and also the diversity of the deities they worship. It makes the statement that there are various types of devotees with different motives, and that there are also numerous deities that can be worshipped depending on the desire and temperament of the devotee.

Human beings are endowed with the power of free will and individual choice. Some people will choose a form of Divinity based on their family tradition, language, religion or culture. Others may do so based on their personal beliefs. It is a personal choice which should be respected. The word "sraddha" refers to the faith of a devotee with which she/he installs, with due ceremony, a picture or an image made of metal, wood, clay or stone and proceeds to do "puja" or worship. The word "sraddham" later in the verse is more specific and refers to that faith or conviction which is directed towards the particular deity selected by the devotee.

As the world becomes more interconnected and interrelated, we're beginning to see that God and spirituality exist in all cultures and religions. Images of Ganesh, Shiva, Virgin Mary, Jesus, and Buddha are found in homes and places of worship all around the world. While each is different, the essence is the same. The search for answers in different ideologies, therapies and wisdoms can take place inside or outside established religions. The spiritual journey is really the process of discovering who you are, what you want and what brings you to those special moments of peace and joy. For some people, the journey is about finding God, and for others, it's simply about finding themselves.

A symbol serves as a focusing tool. If a devotee meditates on a particular image or symbol of a spiritual person or a revered teacher, the devotee becomes attuned to the energy of that teacher, imbibing her/his qualities and feeling the Divinity of that person. In the age of information technology, it is like tuning into the wave frequency of a particular television station, radio station or the database of a website. We gain access to that stream of information and knowledge. Similarly, by focusing and worshipping a great teacher, swami or saint, we can align ourselves with their energy and the Supreme Energy they have aligned themselves with.

When the mind of a devotee is concentrated on a symbol, picture or sculpture representing Divinity, the focused energy is etched and becomes a permanent blueprint in the ether or akashic records. Ether (or space) is one of the five great elements in vedic science and is the medium that facilitates the creation and physical manifestation of things. Sustained thoughts in the human mind act like a focused beam of energy in a certain direction. This verse is giving us the assurance that when there are such sustained thoughts, the Divine Consciousness intervenes and assists in the process. This intervention behaves much like a catalyst and accelerates the process by intensifying and strengthening the faith of that devotee.

UNCONDITIONAL ASSISTANCE

In the Vedic scriptures, the Supreme consciousness is known as **chintamani** or "the jewel that grants all desires". This is an important concept and indicates that the guarantee given by this verse is not selective, it is absolute. Whatever representative form of Divinity is chosen by a devotee will receive the grace of God because Supreme Consciousness is unfathomable. It is omnipresent, omniscient and omnipotent. As human beings, we have the freedom of choice and the capacity to experience the karmic consequences of the various choices we make.

In India we see quite a diverse selection of symbolic forms of Divinity. In Hinduism, the Divine Trinity constitutes the foundation, with Brahma as the Creator, Vishnu, the Preserver and Shiva, the Dismantler. It is a sound working model. Everything we see must be created, needs to be maintained for a while, and is ultimately dismantled. The maintenance portfolio assumes a larger dimension and we see reference to ten incarnations of Vishnu – Matsya (fish), Kurma (tortoise), Varaha (boar), Narasingha (half-man, half-lion), Vamana (dwarf), Parshurama, Rama, Krishna, Buddha and Kalki (incarnation to come). In addition to these representations, we also see the worship of many other deities such as Hanuman (portrayed as a monkey), Ganesh (as an elephant) and Lakshmi (goddess of Light). Nevertheless, the philosophy is monotheistic – these deities are simply different representations of the one Supreme Consciousness, Brahman.

The oneness of Supreme Divinity is well expressed in the Moola Mantra. This "root", or foundation Mantra, is used in various yoga practices for grounding and centering:

Om Sat Chit Ananda Parabrahma
Purushothama Paramatma

Shri Bhagavati Sametha
Shree Bhagavate Namaha
Om Tat Sat. Hari Om Tat Sat.

We invoke the Supreme Creator
who is Truth, Consciousness and Bliss
And who incarnates as the Supreme Soul in human form
As both Divine Mother and Divine Father. I bow to thee.

Human beings have the choice of selecting whatever form of Divinity appeals to them. Peace Pilgrim once said "For light, I go directly to the Source of Light, not to any of the reflections." Sometimes it is easy to get distracted by the finger that is pointing to the sky. When we forge a devotional link with Divinity, it is the nature of Universal Consciousness to support and intensify that connection. It is as if the Universe is in waiting for our first move. The Bengali poet, Rabindranath Tagore expresses it well when he writes:

> God waits to win back his own flowers
> as gifts from man's hands.

Later on in other verses of Chapter 7 in *Bhagavad Gita*, we read that the fruit of such devotion is incremental and cumulative. Every act of reverence is a step forward along our sacred path. Every expression of gratitude is precious. It is a response to the divine spark in all of us. It all adds up and facilitates in the progressive journey towards salvation. In the eyes of a self-realized devotee, the whole world is a manifestation of the Divine.

DISCUSSION QUESTIONS

1. Why are there so many different forms of worship in the world?
2. What form of worship is appealing to you?
3. Does Chapter 7, Verse 21 of Bhagavad Gita contradict the philosophy of any major religion? How and why?
4. What is the responsibility of having free will and individual choice?

INSPIRATIONAL QUOTES

In this world God resides in all things
– *Yajur Veda*

For those with faith, no explanation is necessary.
For those without, no explanation is possible.
– *Thomas Aquinas*

If I had to choose a religion, the sun as the universal
giver of life would be my God.
– *Napoleon Bonaparte*

Within this earthen vessel are bowers and groves,
and within it is the Creator.
Within this vessel are the seven oceans and the unnumbered stars.
Listen to me, my friend.
The beloved Lord is within.
– *Kabir*

The birds have vanished into the sky,
And now the last cloud drains away.
We sit together, the mountain and me.
Until only the mountain remains.
– *Li Po*

EIGHT

Managing the Gates

BHAGAVAD GITA
CHAPTER 8, VERSE 12

Sarva-dvarani samyamya
Mano hrdi nirudhya ca
Murdhny adhayatmanah pranam
Asthito yoga-dharanam

TRANSLATION

sarva- dvarani	all the doors of the body
samyamya	controlling
manah	the mind
hrdi	in the heart
nirudhya	confining
ca	also
murdhni	on the head
adhaya	fixing
atmanah	of the soul
pranam	life force
asthitah	situated in
yoga-dharanam	the yogic situation

MEANING

A person who controls all the doors of the body, confines the mind in the heart center, fixes the life force on the forehead, and practices yoga will achieve salvation.

THE NINE GATES OF THE BODY

We interact with the external environment through the senses of seeing, hearing, feeling, smelling and touching. The five senses are our antenna to the outside world. These are the gateways through which information is downloaded to our human database. In the *Upanishads*, reference is made to the nine gates of the body. These are the mouth, two eyes, two nostrils, two ears, organ of reproduction and organ of excretion. The advice given in this verse is to prudently manage these doors to the body and be selective about the quality and quantity of information that enters. It is for this reason that some devotees often do the following "Angasparsh Mantra". "Anga" means a part of the human body, and "sparsh" means to touch. This is essentially a symbolic body cleansing and purification ritual which can be done before meditation or performing a religious ceremony:

ANG SPARSH

OM *Vangme aasye –astu (touch lips)*
OM *Nasorme praano-astu (touch nostrils)*
OM *Akshorme chakshurastu (touch eyes)*
OM *Karnyorme shrotramastu (touch ears)*
OM *Baahvorme balamastu (touch arms)*
OM *Oorvorme ojo-astu (touch thighs)*
OM *Arishtaani me-angaani, tanustanvaa me saha santu*
(sprinkle water all over the body)

Let my tongue have the ability to speak well
Let my nostrils have the power of inhalation
Let my eyes be healthy

> Let my ears be clear
> Let my arms be strong
> Let my thighs be sturdy
> Let my entire body be full of energy

Verse 12 in Chapter 8 of *Bhagavad Gita* also outlines the preparation that a human being needs to make in order for Divinity to release its blessings. We do our part and the Universe will do its part. This is the eternal relationship between man and God. Our miracles often come from what is already within us. This is why we need to examine and treasure what is in the house. Very often we get preoccupied with the container and we forget the content. In the *Holy Bible*, we are reminded that Jesus fed multitudes of people with two fish and five loaves of bread. The miracle was done with what was already in the basket. We need to have good, raw material to work with and allow the Divine energy to be the catalyst. A student who has been chanting a mantra for years complained to his teacher that the mantra wasn't working. The teacher asked how he knew that, and the student said that nothing was happening. "Keep on doing your work," the teacher replied, "and let the mantra do its work."

KEEPING GUARD

The monitoring of the gateways to the human body is a continuous process. There should be a gap between impulse and response. This is a fast paced and competitive world with all sorts of electronic information coming at us every day from different angles. We need to be grounded and cognizant of what comes in and what goes out. We also need to be aware of the triggers that start our mental processes, and examine how we manage that emotional flow. The poet Kabir gives us some wonderful advice in the following **doha** (two line poetry format):

> *Bura Jo Dekhan Main Chala*
> *Bura Na Milya Koye*
> *Jo Munn Khoja Apna*
> *To Mujhse Bura Naa Koye*

I searched for the crooked,
I couldn't find a single one.
When I searched myself,
I found the crooked one.

Keeping guard is especially important in the early stages of the spiritual journey. The initial phase of the devotional path, for example, usually involves some external form of worship. You may create a personal altar at home with a picture, a candle, an image of a deity or something sacred from nature. You can also perform various rituals with water, flowers, fruits, incense and fire. This keeps the focus as you are developing the inner strength and perseverance to move in further. As you keep going, the **upaguru**, or inner teacher, draws you into the core of your heart and you feel that you have come to a strange but familiar place.

As you travel along the spiritual path, you have to go deeper and experience what Saint John calls "the dark night of the soul". A seed needs to grow its roots in the dark soil before it can blossom forth into sunlight. It is said that the Indian princess Mirabai spent many years wandering in search of Lord Krishna. It took St. Teresa of Avila some 20 years to go through her journey. As she wrote in her autobiography, she couldn't stop flirting with men. Eventually, she understood that these attachments were merely the expression of an inner desire for a divine connection. Gautama Buddha also faced many temptations under the bodhi tree and kept his vigil. Eventually the breakthrough occurred. The approach is to make a strong resolution using the concept of **sankalpa** – firm resolve. When you are firmly grounded in yourself, you can look for empowerment in your own body, breath, mind and consciousness.

INSIDE THE GATES

The rationale for prudently managing the gates of the body is to protect and nurture the gems that lie within the walls. The greatest gift we have from the Divine Source is our unlimited potential. We do have the power within each of us to create our life the way we want it. The diagram below provides a good demonstration of the Upanishadic model of the five **koshas**, or layers, of a human being:

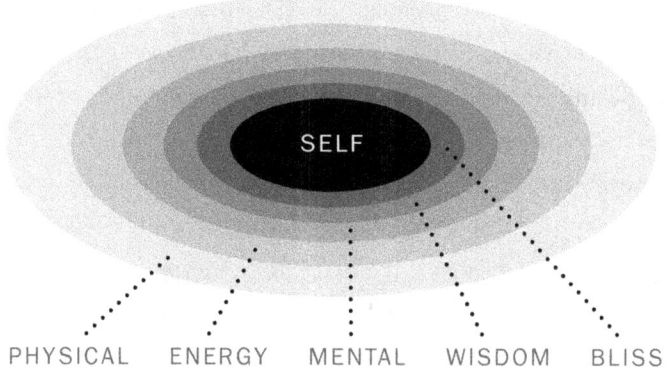

In the innermost concentric circle lies the true Self, the inner core of who we really are. This is where our gems are located. Most of us live our lives around the physical, energy and mental layers. People have a tremendous investment in these outer layers. This is the world we live in. It is where we can build a house and drive a BMW. This is where we dissect things and analyze events with our five sensory perceptions. It takes a lot of courage to venture into the Self. It means shifting your comfort zone. It is like the ocean moving within itself during full moon. Sometimes you need to see that the vices of people are merely steps to the ladder of salvation. It is the process of waking up and reaching in to find out who we really are. When you can see the invisible, you can do the impossible.

The rebel mystic Osho (formerly known as Bhagwan Shree Rajneesh), challenges us to reach for this inner gem by pushing the envelope on our conventional thinking of morality, light, darkness, love and hate. Identifying sex and death as the two great taboos of life, Osho explains that through sex, your body evolved, not you. And through death, your body will dissolve, not you. In one of his more controversial speeches in Pune, he implores us to enjoy with gratitude all that this world has given us, living as if we are Adam and Eve without the shackles of modern religion. His theory is that in living naturally and freely as we are intended, our divine instinct will lead us to the innermost self through our life experiences - good and bad. The inner world is difficult to describe literally. It is often described symbolically so that people from different cultures and social backgrounds can relate to the concept. Some philosophers suggest this is how we should interpret the miracle of Jesus in turning water into wine. The human body is largely water and has a certain lifespan just like grapes. Wine, however, has a much longer shelf life than the grapes from which it is made. It contains the "essence" or "spirit" of the grapes. Thus in converting water into wine, the perishable becomes imperishable.

DISCUSSION QUESTIONS

1. What is the major challenge in guarding the nine gates of the human body?
2. How difficult is the spiritual journey for a professional person living in North America?
3. What behavioural changes occur when someone has realized the existence and importance of the true self?

INSPIRATIONAL QUOTES

> A man sees in the world what he carries in his heart.
> – *Goethe*

> Anyone can hold the helm when the sea is calm.
> – *Unknown*

> Everybody thinks of changing humanity
> but nobody thinks of changing himself.
> – *Leo Tolstoy*

> Not to have control over the senses
> is like sailing in a rudderless ship,

bound to break to pieces
on coming in contact with the very first rock.
– *Mahatma Gandhi*

Have patience with all things,
But more importantly, have patience with yourself.
Each day, begin the task anew.
– *Saint Francis*

The best time to plant a tree was 10 years ago
The second best time to plant a tree is today
– *Old Proverb*

You can never step into the same river twice.
– *Heraclitus*

At any moment you have a choice, that either leads you closer to
your spirit or further away from it.
– *Thich Nhat Hanh*

When you see a beautiful flower in the garden,
Look at its charm. Enjoy its beauty.
Smell its sweet fragrance.
Take a picture next to it.
But don't pluck it from its stem.
Leave it there.
Let it be a beautiful flower for all to enjoy.
– *Author (2002)*

NINE

From the Heart

BHAGAVAD GITA
CHAPTER 9, VERSE 26

Patram puspam phalam toyam
Yo me bhaktya prayacchati
Tad aham bhakti-upahrtam
Asnami prayatatmanah

TRANSLATION

patram	a leaf
puspam	a flower
phalam	a fruit
toyam	water
yah	whoever
me	unto
bhaktya	with devotion
prayacchati	offers
tat	that
aham	I
bhakti-upahrtam	offered in devotion
asnami	accept
prayata-atmanah	whose mind is pure

MEANING

Whoever offers me with devotion a leaf, flower, fruit or water, I will accept.

OFFERINGS

The identification of leaves, flowers, fruits and water as articles of worship indicates that anything which can be easily obtained with minimal expenditure can be used as offerings. Hence the process is accessible to anyone regardless of age, wealth, status or education. The important ingredient in this package is the devotional love from a pure mind. The assurance is given that anyone who offers simple, everyday things to God with a heart filled with love and gratitude can know that they will be accepted.

Medicine men and shamans in different cultures have made offerings to the spirits that guide them. In the Andes, **despacho** is the Quechua word for gift or offering. Among the common things which can be used are fresh fruits, vegetables, tobacco, honey, milk, small coins, grains, nuts and quinoa. The practice is to create a despacho bundle by gathering some of the above ingredients and folding them or tying them in a piece of cloth. After the ritual or ceremony, the despacho bundle is waved around ceremoniously and then burnt.

Throughout history, people have brought various types of offerings to churches and other places of worship to express thanks and seek divine assistance. In Exodus 36: 4-6 of the *Old Testament*, we are told that people kept bringing offerings every morning. So abundant were their gifts that Moses had to ask the people to stop bringing them. *Old Testament* offerings referred to in *the Book of Leviticus* included the various requirements for burnt offerings, grain offerings, guilt offerings and sin offerings. There were also rules about who could partake in those offerings.

Societies have changed over the years and so have the practices around the making of offerings. Buddhists in Thailand make an offering known as **wai phra** which usually consists of a candle, flowers and three sticks of incense. The flowers are placed in water before an image of Buddha and the candle is used to light the incense. Every society and culture in this world has some ceremonial practices around the making of offerings. These practices are culturally specific and are highly symbolic. Some can be elaborate, complex and expensive, while others are remarkably simple. However, at the core of such offerings, we must insert a deep sense of **agape** - pure, unselfish love seeking nothing in return.

SABRI AND SUDAMA

The story of **Sabri** and her wonderful devotion is told in the *Ramayan*. Sabri was a poor woman living in the Dandaka forest who spent her days sweeping the paths to an ashram and gathering wood from the forest. A sage at the ashram was impressed with her hard work and told her that the divine incarnation of Lord Rama would one day visit her cottage and bring her happiness. Expecting the Lord at any moment, she would keep the path to her cottage clean and tidy. She plucked the best fruits from trees in the forest, washed them and kept them in cups intricately made from leaves and flowers. She would repeat this process day after day in preparation for the Divine visit. At last Lord Rama came to her cottage as he was passing through the Dandaka forest on his own life journey. Overwhelmed with joy and love, she was speechless and bowed her head at the feet of the Lord. This story is documented in Goswami Tulsidas's book, *Shree Ramcharitamanas*, and the verses are usually set to melodious music and sung at different Hindu religious festivals. So impressed was the Lord with the simplicity and sincerity of her offering, he later used it as a yardstick and would often remark that good meals were as delicious as the fruits of Sabri.

The story of **Sudama** is narrated in the *Bhagwat Purana*. Sudama was a school friend of Lord Krishna when they both studied at Ujjain with a teacher named Sandipani. After completing school, the two friends parted company and left for their respective homes. Sudama was poor and struggled to provide for his wife and children. His wife knew that Lord Krishna was a childhood friend of Sudama and she asked Sudama to go and request assistance from Lord Krishna in Dvaraka. Sudama was hesitant but, after listening to the pleadings of his wife and considering the plight of his children, he decided to make the trip.

Sudama and his wife searched around the house to find something to take as a gift to Lord Krishna. They could not find anything, so Sudama's wife approached her next door neighbour and was able to get four handfuls of parched rice. She tied this in a piece of cloth and gave it to her husband to take. After a long journey, Sudama reached the city of Dwarka and located the mansion of Lord Krishna. Upon hearing that Sudama had come, Lord Krishna was excited. He left his duties and gave his friend a regal welcome, washing his feet and offering him a nice meal. As they started to chat, Lord Krishna noticed the cloth bundle that Sudama was carrying. He enquired about it, but Sudama was embarrassed about his gift after he saw the royal grandeur of the home. Lord Krishna insisted to see the bundle and as he took it, the cloth tore open and the grains of parched rice fell on the floor.

In beautiful verses, the poet Narottama tells us that the Lord picked up each grain from the floor and began eating them, saying that he hadn't eaten these for a long time. He thanked Sudama for bringing them. After spending a few days with Lord Krishna, Sudama received the good wishes of his friend and returned home. As he approached his old cottage, he saw that it was transformed into a large bungalow with nice amenities. His wife said she woke up one morning and everything had changed. Although they did not discuss it specifically, nor did Sudama ask for anything, Lord Krishna knew the need of his friend and bestowed upon him what he wanted. Sudama and his family lived a comfortable life thereafter, expressing their gratitude for the Lord's blessing.

PURPOSE OF OFFERINGS

A divine offering can be an expression of a prayer, thanksgiving or gratitude. Reverend Cynthia Bourgeault notes that the destiny of any human being is fulfilled in the opening of the heart to the Beloved Divine in each instant. It is this humility and surrender which allows us to be in flow with the Universe, navigating without a safety net and unfolding moment by moment from the core of our being.

There are two ways of approaching the spiritual path – one is to detach completely from society and be a recluse, and the other is to continue your work and earmark regular time slots to maintain a relationship with the Divine Source. The second path is the one that Lord Krishna spoke about in *Bhagavad Gita*. Fighting a war involves a lot of multitasking, concentration and stress. It is also a collective effort and requires good communication skills. If Arjuna can keep his focus on the Divine under such adverse life circumstances, then we can all use his experience as a template in our own lives. Our daily time with God may be limited each day and our offerings may be simple, but if our devotion is sincere then we are assured of divine acceptance.

The best rituals and ceremonies are the simple offerings suggested by Lord Krishna in this verse. Maybe all God wants us to do is to touch a snowflake and watch it melt on our finger. There is a nice Hafiz story that I tell in Yoga Teachers Training lectures. One day a young woman came to see the great 14th century Sufi poet and asked "What is the sign of someone who knows God?" Hafiz looked deeply into the eyes of the young lady and said, "My dear, they have dropped the knife. They have dropped the cruel knife that is often used on their tender self, and on others." In making our humble offerings, we are agreeing to drop the knife and no longer harm ourselves (and others) physically, mentally, emotionally and psychologically. It is letting go and letting God. It is letting the Universal Energy cradle you like the Earth holds the roots of a tree.

DISCUSSION QUESTIONS

1. Why do some people make large offerings in a church or temple?
2. How often should a devotee make divine offerings?
3. Do you think it is appropriate for someone to make offerings on behalf of another person?
4. Is there a common process or approach used in all offerings?

INSPIRATIONAL QUOTES

It is not how much we give, but how much love we put into giving.
– *Mother Teresa*

When eating bamboo sprouts, remember the man who planted them.
– *Chinese Proverb*

A thankful heart is not only the greatest virtue,
but the parent of all other virtues.
– *Cicero*

For us there is only the trying. The rest is not our business.
–*T.S. Eliot*

Happiness resides not in possessions and not in gold,
The feeling of happiness dwells in the soul.
– *Democritus*

He who obtains has little. He who scatters has much.
– *Lao Tzu*

The manner of giving is worth more than the gift.
– *Pierre Corneille, Le Menteur*

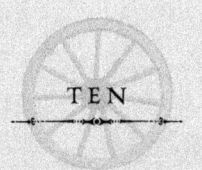

TEN

Source Energy

BHAGAVAD GITA
CHAPTER 10, VERSE 8

Aham sarvasya prabhavo
Mattah sarvam pravartate
Iti matva bhajante mam
Budha bhava samanvitah

TRANSLATION

aham	I
sarvasya	of all
prabhavah	the source of creation
mattah	from Me
sarvam	everything
pravartate	emanates
iti	thus
matva	knowing
bhajante	become devoted
mam	unto Me
budha	the learned
bhava-samanvitah	with great attention

MEANING

I am the Source of creation. Everything emanates from Me. With this realization, the wise become devoted to Me.

AN INTELLIGENT DESIGN

The universal and creative aspects of Divinity have generated much discussion in different cultures. Whether we see a purely intelligent design or a supreme driving force behind the evolutionary theories, there is now a general acceptance of what Father Thomas Keating calls the Divine Seed. If we are made in the image and likeness of God, there must be something of God in us. However, much of this is diluted and distorted by human freedom and human conditioning, so it becomes difficult to recognize this as we grow in self consciousness. But this is the whole purpose of human life. Rabbi Rami Shapiro tells us that the hope is "we are going from the infantilization in the Garden of Eden to Higher Consciousness, where we internalize the Divine and bring it forth into the world." It is true for individuals and also for society.

Living each moment in a divine way seems to go with the flow and allow Universal Energy to experience being human through our life. It is all about giving and receiving love. This seems to correspond with what the Angel Gabriel told Mohammed in the *Hadith*: "I was a hidden treasure desiring to be known. So I created the world." To find the locus of that touch where the divine and the human sides of our life make contact, we need look no further than the human heart. The spontaneous and compassionate impulses of our own wise hearts when they interact with those of others tell a remarkably divine story. The movie *Schindler's List* documents the story of the industrialist Oskar Schindler who risked his life to save people from the gas chambers. It is the divine spark in each human heart that allows the flower of human goodness and kindness to bloom and flourish in such demonic conditions.

There is a fundamental concept in Kashmir Shaivism that God becomes an individual to experience individual uniqueness. The profound joy is to experience yourself and others as divine expressions, living in a space where we experience both similarities and differences, and moving between the two realms without getting stuck in either. The dance of Shiva depicts this flow. In yoga practice, we encourage students to connect from "anahata chakra" and lead from the heart. Extend from the core to the periphery, and create space for your body to breathe. It is how the divine and the human sides connect. Patricia Loring, a prominent Quaker educator, reminds us that "there is God in every person and the connecting point is the human heart. It is the point of change and the point of possibility, and probably the only place where we can meet the Cosmic and know how to change things."

THE SPIDER'S WEB

In the *Vedas*, we are told that the Cosmos evolved like a spider's web from Divine Energy. **Ekam Sat** is a fundamental concept meaning "only one exists". That universal Divine Sutra (thread) is the common fibre which runs through all experiences and all expressions of life and matter on Earth. This creates an interconnectedness and an interdependence of life with the external environment. To the extent that this is so, a sense of balance and harmony represents the natural order of things. Disharmony represents a deviation from this natural state.

As scientific work progresses in this area, we are beginning to see more of a convergence towards the idea of a conscious design theory. Timothy Ferris notes in the *New York Times* that "the search for simplicity is bringing science face to face with the ancient enigma of creation." Ralph Waldo Emerson, the great American writer and lifelong student of Vedic science, notes that the true Doctrine of Omnipresence really means that God exists with all his/her attributes "in every moss and cobweb." Realistically, we can't see the Creator twiddling twenty million atoms, two million quarks and a million leptons in a space lab to create this intelligent Universe as we know it.

There must be a common thread that holds things together. If matter is essentially energy, then everything on Earth is vibrating at one rate or another. As human beings, we often fluctuate between different activities and different states of emotion. When we feel good, we are vibrating in the flow of life and aligned to Source Energy. When we are fearful and angry, we are vibrating at a low energy outside the natural flow of Source. Therefore raising our vibration and connecting to Energy Centre is one way by which we can restore balance and a sense of well being. Essentially, we are all human toys powered by the battery of God.

Writers and poets have pointed to this divine center of energy for years. Hafiz, the Persian poet, captures this nicely in the following verses from *Renderings of Hafiz*:

A GOLDEN COMPASS
Forget every idea of right and wrong
Any classroom ever taught you.
Look at the Perfect One
At the Circle's Centre
He spins and whirls like a Golden Compass
Beyond all that is rational

To show this dear world
That everything in existence
Does point to God.

Kirtan singers and musicians also convey this concept to us in such songs as the following devotional rendering to Lord Krishna:

Mera aapki kripa se, sab kaam ho raha hai
Karte to tum Kanhaiya, mere naam ho raha hai

Patavar kay bina he, mere naav chal rahi hai
Hairaan he zamana, manzil bhi mil rahi hai
Karta nahi hai kuch bhi, sab kaam ho raha hai

Tum saath ho jo mere, kis cheez ki kami hai
Kisi aur cheez ki ab, darkar hi nahi hai
Tere saath se gulam ab, gulfaam ho raha hai

With you compassion, all the work is being done.
You are the Doer, Oh Krishna, and I get the fame.

My boat moves without the rudder and the world is amazed that the destination is found. I didn't do anything, yet everything is done.

When you (Krishna) are with me, what is missing? With your companionship, this slave is turning into a colourful personality.

> **DISCUSSION QUESTIONS**
>
> 1. What is the source of creation?
> 2. How do most people connect with Source Energy?
> 3. What are the greatest obstacles in living a harmonious life?
> 4. Is there something you can do each day to achieve balance in your life?

INSPIRATIONAL QUOTES

I cannot imagine how the clockwork of the Universe can exist without a clockmaker.
If there were no God, it would be necessary to invent him.
— *Voltaire*

If you don't find God in the next person you meet,
it is a waste of time looking for him further.
— *Mahatma Gandhi*

Religion is a guy in church thinking about fishing.
Spirituality is a guy out fishing thinking about God.
— *John Fischer*

Don't look for God in the sky, look within your own body.
— *Osho*

If you are further away from God than you used to be, who moved?
— *Unknown*

ELEVEN

Divine Vision

BHAGAVAD GITA
CHAPTER 11, VERSE 8

Na tu mam sakyase drastum
Anenaiva sva-chasusa
Divyam dadami te chaksuh
Pasya me yogam aisvaram

TRANSLATION

na	never	*divyam*	divine
tu	but	*dadami*	I give
mam	me	*te*	to you
sakyase	are able	*chaksuh*	eyes
drastum	to see	*pasya*	see
anena	with these	*me*	my
eva	certainly	*yogam aisvaram*	unique yogic powers
sva-chaksusa	your own eyes		

MEANING

But you cannot see me with your normal eyes. Therefore, I give you divine eyes. Behold my yogic powers.

Divine Vision

THE REQUEST

Earlier in Chapter 11 of *Bhagavad Gita*, Arjuna pleaded with Lord Krishna to see the cosmic manifestation of Divine Energy. He told Krishna that while he greatly appreciated his valuable advice and his role as the charioteer, he wished to see the universal form of God. By this time Arjuna began to realize that the visible form of Krishna sitting in the chariot and helping him was simply a human form subject to the temporary time of this material world. He wanted to see Krishna in his role as **Yogeswara**, the Lord of the Yogis who has acquired mystical abilities. Supreme Consciousness can have a form and can also be formless. In his form as Yogeswara, Krishna uses his supreme yoga powers and gave Arjuna a glimpse of himself as the Cosmic Creator, the Divine Ruler whose body is the universe.

In reading and discussing this portion of the *Gita*, we may wonder if Arjuna required additional proof or further verification from Krishna about his divine nature. We may also think that he wanted to see some spectacular feature of Divinity to convince others that he indeed received divine wisdom and guidance in the war. This is understandable when we consider the general scepticism in society regarding spiritual issues and divine events. However, many scholars think that Arjuna had a more specific and immediate interest in mind. The idea was seeded when Krishna said "Ask of me anything. Whatever you desire - whether of the past, present or future - it shall appear before you". Arjuna, like most of us, was concerned with the task at hand and its ultimate outcome. He was keenly interested in the outcome of the impending battle on the field at Kurukshetra - who will win?

We are reminded in the *Upanishads* that the Divine is Omniscient and is the reservoir of all knowledge.

> God is omniscient (all-knowing).
> He Himself is the form of knowledge.
> – *Mundaka Upanishad, 1/2/9*

Krishna was clearly aware of Arjuna's unspoken request, just as he was aware of those of Udhava and Sudama. Most humans are naturally curious and would like some indication of future outcomes - hence our interest in astrology, horoscopes and Nostradamus. The important issue seemed to be this. Was the timing right? Was Arjuna prepared for this revelation, and could he now handle knowledge of the results of the war? We should remember that not everyone is prepared to handle the reality of events. The dream may be so nice that we don't want to wake up. It was Jack Nicholson, in his unique dramatic style, who said to Tom Cruise in the movie *A Few Good Men*: "You want answers? You can't handle the truth."

WITH DIVINE EYES

In keeping up with the frantic pace of day to day activity, we tend to miss a lot of the really important stuff in life. Mike Dooley reminds us of the divine call in his book entitled *Notes from the Universe*:

> Hello
> It's me, the Universe.
> I've got good news and bad news
> The good news is that you have passed the audition.
> You're a certified, bonefide Being of Light.

The bad news is that this message
was supposed to reach you eons ago.

Here on the battlefield we have Arjuna with his mental cylinders firing in all directions, trying to strategize and mobilize his army to win. Talk about pressure and stress! Entwined in the immediacy and adrenalin rush of the situation, Krishna decides to talk to him about **sanatan dharma** (the eternal obligation). As Charles Dickens wrote in *A Tale of Two Cities*, "it was the best of times, and the worst of times... the spring of hope, and the autumn of despair." Life on Earth is a workshop. It's where we come to try various things and learn different lessons. In the process, the Divine is always there, guiding us and steering our chariot in the direction necessary for our spiritual advancement.

Having already given Arjuna these lessons, Krishna decides to give him a macro view of things so that he can put that knowledge in perspective. For this Arjuna needed divine vision. This is known in Sanskrit as **divyam chaksu** (divine eyes). It's like been taken up in a helicopter to see an aerial view of the city in which you live, or getting special glasses to view a 3D movie. Wow! What a change in perspective! Arjuna saw the majestic Divine in different glorious manifestations, some compassionate and some fierce. He saw multitudes of spiritual and evil personalities and their destinies. There was the earth, planets, space and multiple universes. Arjuna was petrified.

The lesson in this experience is that human beings have the potential to see the Divine as omnipresent, omnipotent and omniscient. It is available to us. We can ask. "Ask and you will receive" is the guarantee we have been given. We have the power of choice, and when we receive, we then choose what to do with our gift. Unfortunately, this is where a lot of us run into trouble. The ego of a talented singer or a skilled neurosurgeon is so disappointing. How can we not see that this person was chosen as an instrument to convey God's grace for the benefit of human well being. Nothing is permanent, and this person also shall depart. The love and compassion of the Divine will remain.

The yogic faculty of divine vision is described in Vibhutipadah, the third section of Patanjali's *Yoga Sutras*. If the lens is clouded, the object is blurred no matter how good the eye is. Through yoga practice and balanced living, the mind can reach a stage where linkage with an object, external or internal, becomes consistent and continuous, and distractions disappear (**samyama** in Sanskrit). From Verses 17 to 55, Patanjali discusses samyama on the sun, moon, throat, heart, navel etc. as techniques to acquire mastery over the senses and extraordinary abilities. However, these are divine gifts and should be used responsibly. In Kaivalyapadah, the final section of the *Yoga Sutras*, Patanjali emphasizes that the refined mind is still a servant and not a master. If the mind is allowed to assume the dominant role, problems of ego appear and the gifts are misused, bringing adverse consequences.

FISHERMAN TO HOLY MAN

Arjuna's divine experience was direct and magnificent. There are many others which are partial but significant in their own way, like this story about a fisherman.

One magnificent moonlit night, a fisherman climbed the wall of a private estate to partake in the bounty of its fish stocked pond. He moved with stealth and upon reaching the banks of the pond observed with keen alertness that there was no activity in the bungalow nearby. All the lights were out. With an air of confidence, he envisioned his fishing needs taken care of for the week and cast his net into the pond making a light splash.

The master of the house heard a faint sound and woke up his wife, "Did you hear a sound outside?" His wife remarked, "My dear, it sounded like a net falling into the water." In seconds, the owner sprang out of his sleep and visualizing his pond devoid of fish yelled, "THIEF! THIEF!" The servants of the house, hearing the master yell, scrambled outside and headed towards the fish pond.

The fisherman gathered the net as swiftly as he could and scrambled to find a safe hiding place. The workers' voices were nearing and the fisherman's desperation knew no bounds. His eyes caught a glimpse of a smoldering fire nearby and he got an idea. He immediately gathered ash and rubbed it over his arms, body and face (these are metaphorical connections to life's transformations in Hindu beliefs) and he quickly sat under the nearest tree in the posture of someone deep in meditation. When the servants arrived at the scene and saw a man in meditation, they asked for forgiveness and continued their search. Finally, they reported back to the owner to tell him that there was only a sanyasin (holy man) in the garden.

The owner's face was relieved and he asked to be taken to the site of the sanyasin. Upon seeing the sanyasin, he was overjoyed and demanded that the holy man not be disturbed. The fisherman's fear turned to joy, and then to pride as to how smart he was to outwit the entire household. He sat under the tree till the shades of dawn began to sweep across the night sky.

As he was preparing to leave he saw a small procession of people approaching who had heard of the "holy man" appearing from nowhere. Now he could under no circumstances leave. These people had all come from a neighbouring village and with total devotion brought offerings of food, fruit and gold to invoke the blessings of the "holy man".

At that moment the fisherman realized that if, by assuming the role of a holy man, he has received so much respect and good will, how much more respect and good will he would receive if he were to truly be a sanyasin. So the fisherman thief turned in his net, went for training in an ashram and became a true man of God!

DISCUSSION QUESTION

1. What events have opened your vision to the presence of the Divine?

2. How can we experience the grace of the Divine in everyday life?

3. What techniques can you use to sharpen the insight of your mind?

4. Is it difficult to change one's perception of God?

INSPIRATIONAL QUOTES

> How great is God – beyond our understanding.
> – *Job 36:26*

> People see God every day – they just don't recognize Him.
> – *Pearl Bailey*

The intuitive mind is a Sacred Gift
and the rational mind is a faithful servant.
Somehow we have created a society that honours the servant
and forgets the gift.
– *Albert Einstein*

God is one, but he has innumerable forms.
He is the Creator of all and he Himself takes human form.
– *Guru Nanak*

God is like a mirror.
The mirror never changes, but everybody who looks at it
sees something different.
– *Rabbi Harold Kushner*

With the new day comes new strength and new thought.
– *Eleanor Roosevelt*

TWELVE

Bhakti Yoga

BHAGAVAD GITA
CHAPTER 12, VERSE 9

Atha chittam samadhatum
Na saknosi mayi sthiram
Abhyasa yogena tato
Mam icchaptum dhanamjaya

TRANSLATION

atha	if
chittam	mind
samadhatum	to fix
na	not
saknosi	you are able
mayi	upon me
sthiram	steadily
abhyasa yogena	by the yoga of repeated practice
tatah	then
mam	me
iccha	desire
aptum	to get
dhanam jaya	Arjuna, wealthy (spiritually) one

MEANING

If you cannot fix your mind steadily on Me, Arjuna, then seek to reach me through the yoga of repeated practice.

DEVOTIONAL PATH

Each human being is an individual with a unique mixture of physical, mental and emotional characteristics. Since the temperament of people is different, various types of spiritual discipline are recommended as spiritual paths. The term "**abhyasa yogena**" refers to the repetitive efforts we make to keep the mind engaged in a divine state. This approach is well adapted to people whose minds are prone to wandering and dart from one thought to the next. The engagement of the mind by a repetitive sound is the approach in using mantras and chants to keep focus on divine thoughts.

In his *Yoga Sutras*, Patanjali identified the eightfold path of Yoga. The fifth step in the second stage (Niyama - Personal Attributes) is Ishvarapranidhana. The Spiritual Being greater than us all is known as Ishvar. The whole concept of Ishvarapranidhana is that we should offer ourselves and devote all the fruits of our labours to this Higher Consciousness since this is the life force that sustains us all. This act of surrendering to a Supreme Force allows us to detach from the fruits of our actions and allow the universal laws to operate as they should.

Devotion develops from stage to stage. Just as a flower grows, buds and blossoms in a garden, it is advised to develop love slowly in the garden of your heart. In the Shrimad Bhagavatam and the Vishnu Puranas, nine methods of **bhakti** are identified:

1. **Sravana** - hearing stories of God
2. **Kirtana** - singing the glory of God
3. **Smarana** - remembering the name and presence of God
4. **Padasevana** - service at the feet of God

5. **Archana** - worship of God
6. **Vandana** - prostration to God
7. **Dasya** - cultivating the attitude of a servant of God
8. **Sakhya** - cultivating the traits of a friend of God
9. **Atmanivedana** - complete surrender to God

A person can pursue any method of bhakti that appeals to him or her. One method may be very appealing at a younger age and this preference may change as one gets older. What is important is the steadfast faith and devotion.

THE BHAKTI MOVEMENT

Bhakti means devotion. It is an intense love for the Divine and the expression of this love takes various forms. In the Hindu tradition, devotional songs called **bhajans** and **kirtans** are used in the worship of various manifestations of the Divine as depicted in the various **murtis** (images). In the Sufi culture, rhythmic group singing and drumming are heard in their quaawalis, which are beautiful songs in praise of the Almighty. The Sikh tradition uses gurbanis and Christians use hymns and chants in their devotional services to express love and affection for the Divine.

The Bhakti movement has a long history in India. It started in South India and moved north with an emphasis on devotion instead of rituals. It also moved against the caste system and, with its momentum, produced a great body of literature on music, art and dance. The main schools of bhakti are:

Shaivas - those who worship Lord Shiva, and the gods and goddesses associated with him.

Vaishnavas – those who worship Lord Vishnu, and the various incarnations throughout history

Shaktas – those who worship a variety of Gods and Goddesses

The western world got a colourful taste of this practice in 1966 when Swami Prabhupada founded the Hare Krishna movement in the middle of New York City. It focused on the worship of Lord Krishna, the eight incarnation of Lord Vishnu. The movement attracted a lot of attention with the display of orange robes, shaven heads and public chanting of kirtans. Known today as the International Society for Krishna Consciousness (ISKCON), this movement has over 400 branches around the world. It was established to advance the bhakti movement internationally and now publishes the *Bhagavad Gita* and other books in 70 languages. The recommended means of expressing devotional love is to chant the following Maha Mantra (great mantra):

> Hare Krishna, Hare Krishna, Krishna Krishna, Hare Hare
> Hare Rama, Hare Rama, Rama Rama, Hare Hare

This sixteen word mantra is paying tribute to Krishna and Rama, two important incarnations of Lord Vishnu, both of whom are powerful role models in the eastern wisdom traditions. It is usually chanted using a mala – a rosary consisting of 108 beads. The practice is called **japa**.

The bhakti path is a way of strong, passionate love for the Divine. It is strong and it is passionate. Sometimes we tend to see it as unique and slightly obsessive in nature. It has a focus and it has an intent. Many people see it as a way of demonstrating deep devotion and total love for God. It speaks of a mission and a way forward. As Elwood emphasized in the popular movie *The Blues Brothers*, "We're on a mission from God." Bhakti is total love and it is all consuming.

RAIN AND HAIL

The one distinct advantage of **bhakti marg** (devotional path) is that it is the most easy and natural method of connecting with Divine Consciousness. An expression of love is a natural emotion, and it is something we can readily relate to and feel. One concern is that, in its lower forms, it can assume strong passionate emotions and degenerate into hideous acts of fanaticism. It can be the soothing rain or the abrasive hail.

This **nishtha**, or single pointed attachment to one loved person or object, is very often the reason for denouncing everything else. The same person who is kind, honest and loving with those of like opinion can engage in vile deeds when directed against people outside this sub-group. Swami Vivekananda, in his article "Bhakti Yoga", notes that the fanatical fringe elements in Hinduism, Judaism, Islam, Sikhism and Christianity almost always come from the underdeveloped minds walking the lower plains of the bhakti path. In the Ayurvedic diagnostic framework, it is recognized that many people along the bhakti path display **pitta** dominant personality traits. The strategy here is to direct the energy and emotions towards the love and devotion for the Divine.

It is fair to emphasize that this concern only exists in the early stage as the genuine divine connection is being established. When a person's devotion has progressed beyond a certain point, there is little danger of displays of fanaticism. The entire human system is so saturated with love that it is unlikely be used as an instrument of hatred. However, considering this potential concern, Swami Vivekananda recommends a multi-pronged approach to spiritual development. Three things are necessary for a bird to fly - two wings and the tail (as a rudder). Knowledge (jnana) is one wing. Devotion (bhakti) is the other wing, and Yoga is the tail that keeps us in balance.

For those who cannot pursue these three methods, the bhakti path is their way. In focusing on that particular path, we should resist the temptation to see one as the path of possibility and another as the path of potholes. We must keep in mind that rituals, ceremonies and music are important to engage the progressive soul in a world of so many distractions. However, devotion should be seen as one in a series of successive steps in the mental advancement towards self-realization.

DISCUSSION QUESTIONS

1. Why is love such a powerful human emotion?
2. What are some obstacles that impede the flow of unconditional love?
3. Which of the nine methods of bhakti is most appealing to you? Why?
4. Is hate the opposite of love?
5. Could devotional love become obsessive? In what situations?

INSPIRATIONAL QUOTES

What is done out of love always takes place beyond good and evil.
— *Friedrich Nietzsche*

Every man is a builder of a temple called his body.
— *Henry David Thoreau*

Say not "I have found the truth" but rather "I have found a truth".
— *Khalil Gibran*

Everything in your life is there as a vehicle for your transformation.
Use it.
— *Ram Das (Dr. Richard Alpert)*

There are two ways of spreading light.
To be the candle, or the mirror that reflects it.
— *Edith Wharton*

Devotion is not a uniform to be worn on certain days,
and then to be put aside.
— *Shri Sathya Sai Baba*

All souls were created in the beginning and are finding their way
back to whence they came.
— *Edgar Cayce*

THIRTEEN

Divinity Everywhere

BHAGAVAD GITA
CHAPTER 13, VERSE 29

Samam pasyan hi sarvatra
Samavasthitam isvaram
Na hinasty atmanatmanam
Tato yati param gatim

TRANSLATION

samam	equally	*hinasti*	injure
pasyan	seeing	*atmana*	by the self
hi	certainly	*atmanam*	the self
sarvatra	everywhere	*tatah*	then
samavasthitam	equally situated	*yati*	reaches
isvaram	the Supreme Consciousness	*param*	the supreme
		gatim	destination
na	does not		

MEANING

He who is conscious of the omnipresence of Universal Consciousness does not injure the self with the self. That person reaches the supreme destination.

AWARENESS

It is said that a yogi remains awake when everyone else is sleeping. This sense of awareness is the kind of mental alertness that is in tune with the energy of the Divine. It is this energy that keeps the trees growing, the sun shining and the rain falling. In the Hindu trinity, Lord Vishnu is the Preserver, the Maintenance Superintendent of the Universe. He is depicted with four hands holding a conch, a discuss, a mace and a lotus. These symbols represent his ultimate responsibility for Sound (conch), Time (discuss), Power (mace) and Heart (lotus). He is often seen resting on a bed depicted by the powerful coiled serpent **Seshanag**, which represents the sleeping universe with all its potential. Essentially, this is indicating to us that the Divine is everywhere, permeating time and space, head and heart. Lord Vishnu is a source of great inspiration, fortitude and resilience. There is a popular saying in the Hindu culture:

Marnewale kay do haath
Bhajanewale kay chaar haath

The person who wants to kill you has two hands
The person who is protecting you has four hands

The following is a wonderful Polynesian poem outlining our relationship with the environment and our place in the Universe.

My Place in the Universe
The Ocean I see and sail is my Brother
The Wind is my Sister

It brings Hope. It is fresh and new.

The Sky is my Father and my Mother
It is very great.

The Earth is my Ancestors and the past.
I thank the past and look ahead

I am here to use these elements to improve my life
and that of others.
I accept my place in this Universe.

When we recognize our relationship with the Supreme Consciousness and see ourselves as part and parcel of this great Divine Network, our role on Earth becomes clear. We see the importance of being at peace with ourselves, with others, and with the external environment.

LOW HANGING FRUIT

For 15 years in Edmonton, Alberta, I taught a final year University course in Victimology. The course outline includes a study of various types of personal victimization along with the different healing modalities used to address the social, economic and cultural impact of criminal victimization. One of the most problematic areas in the course is the section on auto-victimization, where people abuse and victimize themselves for a wide range of reasons. We are often our own worst enemies. It is amazing how people rationalize the physical and mental torture they inflict upon themselves. It is even more amazing how people will latch on to an event or a belief and perpetuate a victim mentality for years. Since most people are hurt from the outside in, the healing in these cases often need to commence from the inside out.

In the Aboriginal tradition, when someone consumes alcohol, it is believed that she/he offends their spirit or individual soul. As a result, the spirit leaves the body temporarily. This leaves the person at the mercy of their five senses and their decision making becomes impulsive, erratic and dangerous. We become easy targets for our senses and end up doing long term damage to our physical and mental bodies. We often see and experience people who behave so much out of character when they drink alcohol or take drugs. It is as if we are dealing with an entirely different person with different personality traits.

When the self turns upon the self, it impedes spiritual progress. To be aware of the universal presence of God is to recognize that we are ourselves a part of that huge mosaic of Divine Energy. It is also important to recognize that, as human beings, we are works in progress. In his Essays on Philosophy and Yoga, the Indian writer and poet Sri Aurobindo expresses it as follows:

Man is a transitional being. He is not final.

The step from man to Superman is the next approaching achievement in the earth evolution. It is inevitable because it is at once the intention of the inner spirit and the logic of nature's process."

Each day we change the way we think and approach different situations. It is a gradual awakening process. When we look deeply and compassionately at how we are affecting ourselves and others with our words and actions, we can acknowledge what is happening inside us. The acknowledgement is one step and managing the necessary change is another step. Pema Chodron, the Buddhist nun, tells us that the traditional Zen way is to find the middle path between the extreme views of indulging - going right ahead and telling people off verbally and mentally; and repressing - biting your tongue and turning on yourself.

KEEPING THE FAITH

God has been perceived as the unknown Almighty in many religions and cultures. The heavens declare His glory and the skies proclaim His work. This is the one we call upon in prayer as our loving merciful Saviour. To see Divinity everywhere really means to see the good qualities in all people and things around us. It also means to experience the Presence through the natural environment and see His divine fingerprints in the mountains, rivers and landscape.

As human beings, we have a responsibility to use this Earth in a careful and responsible manner. Our power of choice results in decision making that is often propelled by greed and material gains. Natural disasters, personal challenges and man's injustice to man severely challenge our belief in the role, existence and mercy of God. Nevertheless, through the worst of situations positive things and good outcomes emerge, as if to reinforce our faith in the omnipotence and omniscience of Divine Consciousness. We have this assurance from the Bible.

> Behold, I am the Lord, the God of all flesh.

Is there anything too hard for me?
Jeremiah 32:27

DISCUSSION QUESTIONS

1. Why is self injury so prevalent in our society?

2. How difficult is it to see Divinity everywhere?

3. In what situations do you question the mercy of God?

4. How do you assess the spiritual progress you have made?

INSPIRATIONAL QUOTES

If you can't see God in all,
You can't see God at all.
— *Yogi Bhajan*

Having a wider heart and mind
is more important than having a larger house.
— *Cheng Yen*

The way is not in the sky
The way is in the heart.
— *Buddha*

He who is filled with love is filled with God himself.
— *Saint Augustine*

All you can teach is understanding.
The rest comes on its own.
– *Nisargadatta Maharaj*

Everything in life is speaking in spite of its apparent silence.
– *Hazrat Inayat Khan*

My calamity is my providence
Outwardly it is fire and vengeance
but inwardly, it is light and mercy.
– *Baha'u'llah*

FOURTEEN

The Three Gunas

BHAGAVAD GITA
CHAPTER 14, VERSE 5

Sattvam rajas tamah iti
Gunah prakriti sambhavah
Nibadhnanti maha-baho
Dehe dehinam avyayam

TRANSLATION

sattvam	the mode of goodness	*nibadhnanti*	conditions
rajas	the mode of passion	*maha-baho*	O mighty
tamah	the mode of ignorance	*armed*	One
iti	thus	*dehe*	in this body
gunah	human qualities	*dehinam*	the living
prakriti	material nature		entity
sambhavah	consisting of	*avyayam*	eternal

MEANING

Material nature consists of three modes – **sattva** (goodness), **rajas** (passion) and **tamas** (inertia). When someone comes in contact with nature, O mighty armed Arjuna, she/he becomes conditioned by these three modes.

THREE CATEGORIES

The Sanskrit word "**guna**" literally means a strand of a rope or a cord. The three gunas of this material world are seen as three intertwined strands of a binding rope. It is this rope that binds most human beings and keeps them in bondage in this material world. In this fashion, the perfect soul appears as the distorted ego when it is reflected in one of these modes of nature. This is called maya or the illusion inherent in creation of a human life form. The purpose of human life is to ascend spiritually, and not to be tied down to this material sphere.

Sattva is goodness or purity. It is a quality we all admire. There are some people on Earth who are inherently kind, compassionate and loving. In the case of others, their good deeds sometimes create a feeling of being better than others and their many charitable actions are ultimately performed for the purpose of attaining name, fame or ego gratification. Often the works of great scientists, priests, philosophers and humanitarians fall into this category. Although a sattvic quality is a noble and admirable one, Paramahansa Yogananda explained that "**a gold wire can tie a man to a post just as securely as a wire of silver or steel**." In its inherent nature, sattva also binds the soul to the body and to this material plane on Earth.

Rajas is the mode of passion or thirst for material acquisitions. It is the life of multitasking and wealth accumulation – home of the go getter A- type personality. Unfortunately, this is the arena in which most of us dwell because success and status in the modern world is defined by such criteria. It is not the acquisition, per se, that defines this state, but more so the obsession with acquiring material things. In this state, a person is never satisfied with the position or financial resources she/he has acquired. The mind is occupied with thoughts of increasing and surpassing profit margins and financial targets. It defines much of the material we teach in business schools and MBA programs. The danger is that there is no cessation to this passion with some people. It is overwhelming. As a result of the endless desires this generates, many people leave this world feeling unfulfilled. There is no end to the sense gratification until sometimes, a life altering event occurs to change that perspective.

Tamas is the state of lethargy and indulgence of the senses. It defines a lifestyle of sinking towards the three lower chakras (lumbar, sacral and coccygeal) and disengaging from the world of activity and spiritual effort. This is the world where people live for "cookie, nookie and snookie." In this specific mode we find drug addicts, alcoholics, and sex-obsessed individuals - people living in a state of inertia, as if they exist in a fogged state of mind in a whole different universe. People in this material mode also harbour twisted perceptions based on their mental states, like the man who mistakes the rope for a snake and behaves accordingly. The common behavioural traits are usually a lack of self control, impulsiveness, arrogance and contempt for advice and guidance.

After Lord Krishna explained these three modes of material nature, Arjuna asked him about rising beyond the bondage of the three gunas. Krishna provided a simple and direct response - complete devotion to God so that one's mind has no room for thought of the self.

THE BANYAN TREE

There is a wonderful analogy of the banyan tree provided in the *Bhagavad Gita*. The Banyan tree, ficus indicus, branches out in all directions, draws nutrients from its many roots, and spreads out its branches far and wide. Yet it stems from one single great trunk. It is a highly symbolic tree in Eastern philosophy. It is also regarded like the pipal or the holy fig tree. In Hindu culture it is widely considered sacred and is called "**kalpa vriksha**", the wish fulfilling tree. Buddha is believed to have achieved enlightenment in Bodhgaya, India while meditating under a banyan tree now known as the Bodhi tree.

As a tree is nourished by water, so is the banyan tree nourished by the three modes of material nature – **sattva**, **rajas** and **tamas**. The expansive branched system represents the integrated consciousness, life force and the various nerves that make up a human being. The twigs and leaves of the tree are considered to be sense objects which receive and transmit different sensations. The one giant root is symbolic of the Divine Source and the subsidiary roots are attachments and aversions, which are the by-products of different varieties of sense enjoyment and suffering.

In esoteric literature, the phenomenon of the inverted tree is used to explain the human body and how we should function in this world. If you turn the chart of the nervous system upside down with the feet above and brain below, you will see the similarity to a tree with its trunk and branches. The reflection of a tree in water also gives one the image of the roots in heaven and the branches in this material world. If we are nourished by thoughts in the spiritual realm, the manifestation of our

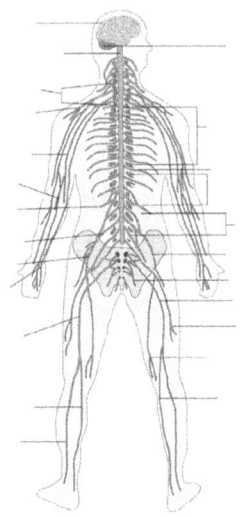

words and actions on Earth will be kind, compassionate and loving. It's a matter of perception as William Blake writes in *The Marriage of Heaven and Hell* and later explaining that "a fool sees not the same tree as a wise man does".

PERSONAL TRANSFORMATION

We must recognize that human beings, created in the image of God, are capable of remarkable transformation, both individually and collectively. So are families, communities and countries. As I am writing this chapter on February 11th, 2011, the world is witnessing the transformation of Egypt from a totalitarian regime. With a population of 84 million people, Egypt is the most populated country in the Arab world. It has had a long history of being ruled by pharaohs and military strongmen. Mobilized by the social networking of young people, thousands of Egyptians articulated their dissatisfaction in Tahrir Square. Played out in front of non-stop global television coverage, it took exactly eighteen days of well coordinated effort and protests by the people of Egypt to bring the 30 year old regime of President Hosni Mubarak to an end. The collective effort focused on the principle of "**Satyagraha**", the principle of non-violence used by Mahatma Gandhi to free India from 300 years of British rule.

In spite of the restraints created by the three gunas, human beings can transform themselves. It is something I firmly believe in, probably indicative of my faith in the divine component of human beings. **After all, as Swami Vivekananda tells us, we are spiritual beings having a material existence at this time.** People can progress materially and spiritually. It does not mean that because you are progressing financially you cannot progress spiritually. A person can move ahead spiritually in any socioeconomic environment. A lotus grows out beautifully from the murkiest of waters. A lot of the spiritual institutions today would not exist if it were not for the foresight and benevolence of some kind-hearted, wealthy people. There is an inherent balance in this dynamic. The ability to learn from the lessons of life experiences, recalibrate and move forward on the spiritual path is an avenue open to us all. Some choose to seize that opportunity and some do not.

Wayne Dyer, the popular author and lecturer, explains that the way to effect deep spiritual change is to work at allowing the highest part of you, the invisible part of you, the divine part of you, to become the dominant force in your life. It is done by getting quiet and becoming peaceful. You have to use the mind to lose the mind. This essentially shuts down the inner dialogue. In the process of losing the mind, you make conscious contact with the Divine energy.

Stories of personal self transformation are quite inspiring. Seeing the upside down tree means a shift in perspective where the purpose of human life becomes apparent and daily activities assume their appropriate role in the whole spectrum of things. Certainly the biggest challenge here is the retooling of behaviours which may have served the individual so well in advancing his/her career or social status. Here is a brief description of three models of personal and spiritual transformation:

1. **Triple Transformation Model**

This is a model from Shri Aurobindo and the Integral Yoga School. With the consistent practice of Yoga, the subtle energy centres of the body (chakras) become activated. The three gunas (modes of Nature) which constitute the consciousness become purified and change into their divine equivalents.

    A. **Sattva** (purity) becomes Jyoti, the authentic Spiritual Light.
    B. **Rajas** (passion) becomes Tapas, the intense Divine Force.
    C. **Tamas** (lethargy) becomes Sama, the Divine peace and tranquil.

2. The Archetypal Model

One of the most recent archetypal models is the one outlined by Carolyn Myss in her book *Sacred Contracts*. Utilizing knowledge of the major chakras in the subtle energy system of the human body, it provides an analysis based on archetypal classifications.

Each person is born with a sacred contract which is a Divine Agreement to learn certain lessons and develop wisdom in this lifetime. We all share four survival oriented archetypes and there is a set of twelve archetypes which helps us to pursue this required wisdom. The model explains a process of identifying and exploring these archetypes in order, so that you can learn about the energies which help and hinder you in your spiritual journey.

3. The Appreciative Inquiry Model

This is a high energy process which facilitates the philosophical shift of focusing on the positive and possible outcome instead of the problematic. It seeks to awaken the dormant passions and enthusiasm in an individual.

Using the lens of attraction rather than that of resistance, a person begins the process of identifying a new attractor to move them away from the existing attractors. The Chart on the following page identifies the five stages of the Model. The Revelation phase is where the person explores the current attractors. Then an affirmation is made and a role model selected to explore and connect the person to what new talents, beliefs, habits and emotions the role model developed in a ten year period of their personal growth.

The process also involves a reframing of your current situation to explore the inner skills, talents and strengths you already possess. The idea is to connect this with the affirmation stage to get to the exploration and experimentation of the new thoughts and behaviours. If you encounter problems at any stage, the Model teaches you to "fail" forward so that you can take a step back, recalibrate and still move ahead in your journey of personal transformation.

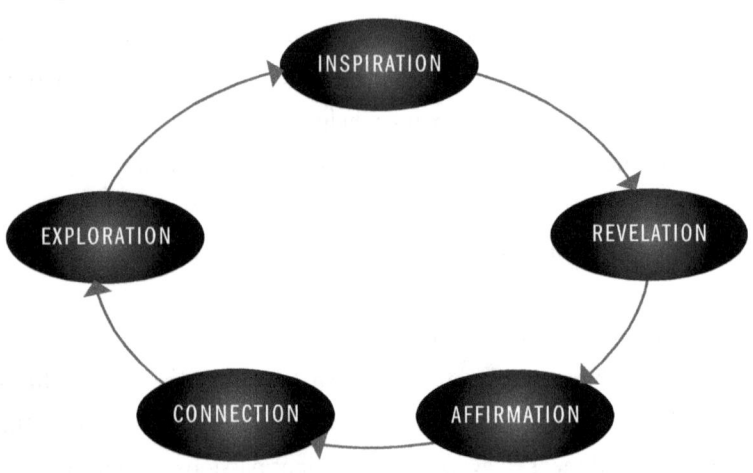

THE FIVE STAGE APPRECIATIVE INQUIRY MODEL

DISCUSSION QUESTIONS

1. Is a sattvic person still attached to the material world. Why?
2. What is so attractive about the rajasic mode of nature?
3. Could someone change from one material mode to the next?
4. How can you free yourself from the restraint of the three gunas?

INSPIRATIONAL QUOTES

Emancipation from the bondage of the soil
is no freedom for the tree.
– Rabindranath Tagore

Bondage is of the mind,
Freedom too is of the mind,
If you say I am a free soul, free you shall be.
– Ramakrishna

The moment I have realized God sitting in the temple
of every human body,
The moment I stand in reverence before every human being
and see God in him,
That moment I am free from bondage,
everything that binds vanishes, and I am free.
– Swami Vivekananda

Religious bondage shackles and debilitates the mind
and unfits it for every expanded prospect.
– *James Madison*

Life is not a race but a journey to be savoured every step of the way.
– *Author*

Whatever exists and wherever it exists
is permeated by the same Divine power and force.
– *Yajur Veda*

Any ritual is an opportunity for transformation.
– *Starhawk*

FIFTEEN

Prana Vayus and Digestive Fire

BHAGAVAD GITA

CHAPTER 15, VERSE 14

Aham vaishvanaro bhutva
Praninam deham asritah
Pranapana samayuktah
Pachamy annam chatur vidham

TRANSLATION

aham	I
vaisvanarah	digesting fire
bhutva	becoming
praninam	of all living entities
deham	in the bodies
asritah	situated
prana	inward moving air
apana	the downward moving breath
samayuktah	keeping in balance
pachamy	I digest
annam	food
chatur vidham	eaten in the four ways

MEANING

Becoming the digestive fire, I exist in all living creatures, and through prana and apana, I digest foods eaten in the four ways.

PRANA VAYUS

Each human being is a multi layered amalgam of physical and mental wiring specifically designed for our particular soul. We came on this Earth to experience a variety of situations and challenges in order to grow and evolve spiritually. Each step of the way, the Divine is present to assist us. In a person's digestive system, the Divine Energy exists as Vaishvanara, the internal fire that facilitates the process of digestion. It works with the vital energy streams to sustain life.

Working in conjunction with the flow of prana, life is sustained by the life force which is extracted from food in the following four ways:

1. Mastication (of solid foods)
2. Sucking (of liquid substances)
3. Licking (food eaten with the tongue)
4. Swallowing (ingestion of oxygen from breathing)

Prana is the basic life force, the master form of energy working at the physical, mental and spiritual levels. It is the creative power and the power of Divinity within each of us. The main role of prana is to connect different parts and link things together. In his book *Yoga and Ayurveda*, David Frawley notes that "even **kundalini shakti**, the serpent power or inner force that transforms consciousness, develops from the awakened prana." The one primary stream of prana divides itself into five types according to its movement and direction. They are called prana vayus or powers of air.

1. **Prana Vayu**
This is the forward and inward moving air. It facilitates the eating of foods, drinking of liquids and inhalation of air. It provides the basic energy for us and nourishes the brain.

2. **Apana Vayu**
It is the downward moving air. It regulates the elimination of stool and urine and the expulsion of semen and menstrual fluids. It is the vital energy of the abdomen that allows for the process of elimination and reproduction.

3. **Udana Vayu**
This is the upward moving air. It pertains to the growth of the human body and speech, allowing us to stand confidential. It is the vital energy in the throat that governs speech and self expression.

4. **Samana Vayu**
This means the balancing air. It moves around the centre of the body in a churning kind of action and assists with digestion. Samana does its work in the gastrointestinal tract to digest food and in the lungs to digest air and absorb oxygen.

5. **Vyana Vayu**
It is the outward moving air working form the centre to the periphery. It regulates the circulatory system and moves oxygen, food and water around the body. This is the vital energy force in the heart and lungs.

Recognizing the role and importance of the prana vayus, there is a short ritual that devotees and yogis use at mealtime. Before eating, some water is sprinkled around the food to purify it while chanting the sound OM. Then the following mantra is chanted to acknowledge the power of the vayus, each time taking a bit of food in your mouth.

OM Pranaya Swaha
OM Apanaya Swaha
OM Udanaya Swaha
OM Samanaya Swaha
OM Vyanaya Swaha

THE AYURVEDA APPROACH

Ayurveda means the knowledge of life (**ayur**-life, **veda**-knowledge). Ayurveda is a holistic approach to health which is designed to help people live long, healthy and well balanced lives. It has been practiced in India for over 5000 years and has recently become popular in western cultures. The basic principle in Ayurveda is to prevent and treat illnesses by maintaining balance in the body, mind and consciousness through proper diet, lifestyle and the use of herbal remedies. Ayurveda and Yoga have existed as sister sciences for thousands of years as a complete healing modality. They address our entire nature and our greater life as a spiritual being in a physical body.

According to Ayurveda, there are three primary energies, or Doshas. The Doshas are **Vata**, **Pitta**, and **Kapha**. These Doshas regulate all physical and psychological behaviours, from basic cell structure to the most complex mental functions. The Doshas are found in unique proportions in every individual. This combination of the

Doshas is called our constitution or Prakriti, and it will determine our basic physical appearance, preferences, behaviours, and emotional tendencies. When the Doshas are in their natural balance with one another, our physical and mental states are at optimum health. When the Doshas fall out of balance, disease may manifest. Ayurveda treatment seeks to return and maintain the Doshas at their natural balance in our individual constitution.

According to the *Charaka Samhita*, the Ayurvedic therapies depend on the status of the doshas. For example:

- If the disease is new and the aggravated doshas are not very strong, fasting by itself may be sufficient to restore health.
- If the doshas are medium in strength, specific medicines are used to induce balance inside the body. This type of therapy is termed as **shamana** therapy.
- If the disease is in a chronic stage and the dosha aggravation is strong, **shodhana** therapy is applied to eliminate the excess dosha from the body.

Many people today go for **panchakarma** ayurvedic treatments at spas and wellness centres. Panchakarma means five purification practices. The process usually follows a preparation treatment of oil massage (**snehana**) and steam therapy (**svedana**) to loosen the toxins and move them to the digestive tract for their removal. Panchakarma can be done as part of a detoxification program or on a regular basis to prevent toxins from accumulating in the body. The different treatments work by increasing **apana vayu** to reduce pitta imbalance, stimulate **udana vayu** to reduce **kapha**, and calm **apana vayu** to reduce vatta. In this way the process removes toxins from both the physical and the subtle body and assists in maintaining good health.

PSYCHEDELIC SWAMIS

The revolutionary body, mind and spirit movement which transformed American and Western society actually got its start in academic circles in conservative Boston, Massachusetts in the 1960's. Much of its philosophy and principles were imported from the eastern cultures of India and Tibet. It was around this time that many people started to actively explore the world of Yoga and Ayurveda, experimenting with the sounds and taste of Indian culture.

It was in Cambridge and Newton that the fertile seeds were planted in the west. Four men - Timothy Leary, a Harvard research psychologist; Dr. Richard Alpert (better known as Ram Dass, the name he adopted after a rather enlightening trip to India), a Harvard Psychology Professor; Huston Smith, an MIT Philosophy Professor and Dr. Andrew Weil, then a Harvard medical school student, launched what would eventually become the counter culture movement. Through their trailblazing experimentation with hallucinogenic drugs, this *Harvard Psychedelic Club* influenced everything from literature, music and movies to the rise of the Silicon Valley technology sector in California. Today their influence extends to what we eat, how we exercise and our psychological perceptions of ourselves.

Throughout the 1960's and 1970's, a steady stream of westerners travelled to India to pursue yoga, ayurveda, meditation and spiritualism. The focus was the exploration of vedantic philosophy and the rituals and ceremonies associated with the various Gods and Goddesses in Hinduism. A number of westerners studied with Neem Karoli Baba, a Bhakti yogi and mystic teacher in North India. Others gravitated to the ashrams of Rishikesh after the popularized visit of the Beatles. A number of hippie communities bonded with the "Naga" tradition and found that they had something in common – the use of psychoactive plant materials to induce enhanced states of consciousness. Near the burning ghats at Varanasi, a huge commune grew up around the charismatic Ganesh Baba and his liberal teachings.

It is clear that these spiritual seekers pushed the envelope on a number of issues, but many of them returned to the West as vehicles of this spiritual knowledge. Whether we agree with their lifestyle or their marketing of this information, or whether we see this as spiritual materialism, they lit the torch. Today, meditation and yoga classes are in every North American and European city. Various translations of the *Bhagavad Gita* have made their way into bookstores and universities in the western world. The teachings of Krishna are now explored at various discussion groups, almost metaphorically endorsing the notion that the Divine Energy exits as the digestive fire in all living beings, digesting foods eaten in any manner.

DISCUSSION QUESTIONS

1. What were the 1960's spiritual seekers hoping to find in India?
2. Why is vyana vayu so important in maintaining good health?
3. How can you use Ayurvedic principles to better manage your health?
4. What human behaviors arise from toxic emotions?
5. How does a person begin to heal from emotional trauma?

INSPIRATIONAL QUOTES

The greatest wealth is health.
— *Virgil*

Every human being is the author of his/her own health or disease.
— *Buddha*

Our health always seems more valuable after we lose it.
— *Author*

It is health that is real wealth, not pieces of gold and silver.
— *Mahatma Gandhi*

I am going to drink, to dance, to love
Because I trust God is compassionate - he will forgive.
— *Omar Khayyam (Rubaiyat)*

Great spirits have always encountered violent opposition from mediocre minds.
— *Albert Einstein*

SIXTEEN

The Dark Side

BHAGAVAD GITA
CHAPTER 16, VERSE 21

Tri-vidham narakasyedam
Dvaram nasanam atmanah
Kamah krodhas tatha lobhas
Tasmad etat trayam tyajet

TRANSLATION

tri-vidham	three kinds	*krodhah*	anger
narakasya	of hell	*tatha*	as well as
idam	this	*lobhah*	greed
dvaram	gates	*tasmat*	therefore
nasanam	destructive	*etat*	these
atmanah	of the self	*trayam*	three
kamah	lust	*tyajet*	one must abandon

MEANING

There are three gates to hell – lust, anger and greed. Therefore, one must abandon these as they are destructive to the spirit.

THE MATERIAL LIFE

Much of daily living consists of satisfying our material needs. Without the benefit of material things, we are unable to have food, clothing, shelter and the means to move around. The material side of worldly living is an important one but it can be a stumbling block on the path to happiness. Material things can satisfy our desires, but such satisfaction is often short lived. Before long, the whole cycle of wanting, striving and acquiring starts all over again. If we look for happiness in material things, we are destined for disappointment.

There is a popular method of catching monkeys on the islands in the Indian Ocean. After drilling a small hole into a coconut, they empty out the water and stuff some of the monkeys' favourite food inside. Later, attracted by the smell of food, a monkey squeezes its hand through the hole, grabs the food, and then discovers it cannot pull its enlarged fist out of the hole. Why doesn't it just drop the food and try again? The greedy monkey doesn't want to let go of the food! While the bewildered monkey is trying to figure out how to remove the coconut from its hand, it is quickly captured with a net. Like the monkey, we can become prisoners of our own greed and slaves to our own addictions.

Let's suppose we acquire a very expensive object. The minute that thing comes into our possession, our mind changes. We start to think "Now, where can I keep it? If I leave it there, it could be lost or somebody might steal it." We get into a state of worry trying to find a place to keep it safely and preserve its value. And when did the mind change? It changed the minute we obtained that object. If we continue to follow a social model that is conditioned by money, possessions and power, we will live in a constant state of fear, tension and anxiety. This is a myopic view of life that inhibits the accumulation of spiritual knowledge. It also feeds the flames of anger, greed and lust.

THE LOWER CHAKRAS

The Sanskrit word chakra means a wheel. The chakra system is a series of wheel-like vortices which exist in the subtle body. This invisible part of the physical body is of great importance to us. It is the vehicle through which flows the streams of vital energy which keep the body alive and healthy. This structure acts as a bridge to convey undulations of thoughts and feelings from the astral to the visible. The chakras or awareness-centres are points of connection from which energy flows from the subtle body to the physical body. When undeveloped, they appear as small circles about two inches in diameter, with a dull glow. When awakened, they are seen as blazing miniature suns much increased in size.

All chakras correspond to certain physical organs. They absorb, digest, and distribute **prana** to the different parts of the body. They control, energize, and are responsible for the proper functioning of the whole physical body and its different parts and organs. For example, the endocrine glands are controlled and energized by some of the major chakras. The endocrine glands can be stimulated or inhibited by controlling or manipulating the corresponding chakras. Many physical and emotional ailments can be caused by blockages of these chakras. Some chakras are sites of the psychic faculties and activation of those chakras may result in the development of certain psychic faculties. For example, if you activate certain chakras you develop the ability to feel subtle energies and the ability to feel outer energies, health and auras. Through the consistent practice of yoga, those chakras are activated and some of these abilities can be acquired. These are described in detail by Patanjali in Vibhutipada, the third section of *The Yoga Sutras*.

The seven (7) upper chakras, from lowest to highest, are:
1. Muladhara chakra (base of spine) – memory, time and space.
2. Svadhishthana chakra (below navel) – reason.
3. Manipura chakra (solar plexus) – willpower.
4. Anahata chakra (heart center) – direct cognition.
5. Vishuddha chakra (throat) – divine love.
6. Ajna chakra (third eye) – divine sight.
7. Sahasrara chakra (crown of head) – illumination, divinity.

There are also seven lower chakras. From highest to lowest, they are:
1. Atala chakra (hips) – fear and lust.
2. Vitala chakra (thighs) – anger.
3. Sutala chakra (knees) – greed and jealousy.
4. Talatala chakra (calves) – mental confusion.
5. Rasatala chakra (ankles) – selfishness.
6. Mahatala chakra (feet) – absence of conscience.
7. Patala chakra (located in the soles of the feet) – malice.

The network of lower chakras is the reservoir of some very toxic thoughts and emotions. Anger, for example, is not bad or good in itself. It is the life force streaming through us like a river in the spring – full of power and purpose. This vital essence within us is very important.

7 Chakras by Pieter Weltevrede

7 CHAKRAS
by Pieter Weltevrede
www.sanatansociety.com

Like the green shoots pushing through the frozen soil, we want to have the ability for the upward and forward movement. We want to express ourselves with clarity, purpose and exuberance.

However, if our lower chakras, especially the chakra at the thighs and the base of the spine that connects us directly to the Earth is wounded and closed off, "the river" of vitality, unable to circulate through the body, will stagnate. This vital power will turn against our self: anger turned inwards. Physically we will suffer from ailments like inflammation, gastrointestinal disorders and anorexia, etc. Mentally, we are literally holding on to anger, irritability, frustration and neurosis. On the other hand, we may resign from life, and experience complete lack of anger and victim mentality, feeling lethargic and depressed. Letting go of anger is one of the best things we can do for our self.

MANAGING ANGER

Anger is a natural and forceful emotion. We encounter anger at home, at work, in social circles and even in church. The bottom line is that anger is contagious and destructive and we should all make an effort to prudently manage this emotion. Patanjali writes about five states of the mind in his *Yoga Sutras*. The fifth state is known as nirodha. This is where the mind is devoid of all vrittis or mental afflictions. Although difficult to achieve, it should be our focal point and define the path we travel in life.

In his May 2007 article on anger, Swami Atmavikasananda notes that there are several adverse effects of anger:

1. We forget the lessons in wisdom learnt in life.

2. We lose the ability to discriminate between right and wrong.
3. We lose control over our thoughts and emotions.
4. We become overactive, with our ego in charge.
5. We become aggressive – verbally and physically.
6. We destroy friendships and relationships.

We cannot avoid anger completely but we can minimize its impact. Here are some practical suggestions to assist you in managing anger:

1. Cultivate the consistent practice of yoga, deep breathing and meditation.
2. At the beginning of each day, spend 15 minutes alone and center yourself and your thoughts.
3. Listen more. When you speak, focus more on the issue, not the person.
4. Develop a sense of humour. Try to see the lighter side of things.
5. Develop consideration for others. We are all different. Try to understand why people think, speak and behave the way they do.
6. Try not to jump to conclusions. Between black and white are varying shades of grey.

Sometimes it helps to chant the following *Universal Prayer for Peace* (Shanti Mantra) to create harmonious vibrations around us and induce a sense of peace and harmony.

Universal Prayer for Peace

Om Dyau Shanti, Antariksha Gwam Shanti
Prithivi Shanti, Rapah Shanti
Aushadhaya Shanti
Vanaspatya Shanti
Vishwa Devah Shanti
Brahma Shanti
Sarvaygwam Shanti
Shanti Reva, Shanti Sama, Shanti Redhi

Let there be peace in the Sky
Let there be peace in the Atmosphere
Let there be peace on Earth
Let there be peace in the Waters
Let there be peace in the Medicinal Herbs
Let there be peace in the Vegetation
Let there be peace with Divine Beings
Let the Creator have peace, and let there be peace everywhere.

THE STORY OF TWO NEIGHBOURS

There were two neighbours living in a village in India - a greedy man and a jealous man. As the greedy man acquired more property and wealth, the jealous man became increasingly restless and angry. One day he noticed that he had not seen his neighbour, the greedy man, for several days. The man seemed to have disappeared.

He asked a few people around the village and eventually found out that the greedy man had taken off to a Shiva temple nearby and has been meditating there for the last few several days. The jealous man immediately went there and started to meditate on Lord Shiva.

As their intense meditation continued day after day, Lord Shiva became very impressed with both of them. This continued for a while and one day Lord Shiva appeared in person and addressing the jealous man, he said, "I am happy with your devotion. I will grant to you anything you desire. It can be anything – land, money or even a kingdom. Whatever you want will be yours."

The jealous man was thrilled and was thinking about what to ask for when Lord Shiva added, "There is just one condition. Whatever you ask for, I will give you, but I will also grant twice that to your neighbour."

The jealous man became concerned. How could he possibly tolerate his greedy neighbour receiving twice his blessings or wealth? He started to think hard for a solution.

A few hours passed, and no request came forth. Finally, Lord Shiva announced that he has to leave soon and needed the request. The jealous man looked at Lord Shiva and said, "Thank you so much, Lord. You are very kind and generous. All I want from you is one blind eye."

DISCUSSION QUESTIONS

1. What can you do to release toxic emotions stored in the human system?
2. Is the pursuit of material comforts an obstacle in spiritual life?
3. Why is anger such a destructive human emotion?
4. What human behaviors arise from toxic emotions?
5. How does a person begin to heal from emotional trauma?

INSPIRATIONAL QUOTES

Lust is the craving for salt of a man who is dying of thirst
— *Frederick Buechner*

The winds of anger blow out the lamp of intelligence.
— *Indian proverb*

Anger is only one letter short of danger.
— *Unknown*

The Earth provides enough to satisfy every man's need,
but not every man's greed.
— *Mahatma Gandhi*

Anger is momentary madness,
so control your passion or it will control you.
— *Horace*

Many go fishing all their lives
without knowing that it is not fish they are after.
— *Thoreau*

Do not associate with those whose hearts are filled with anger.
— *Guru Ram Das*

When you row another person across the river, you get there yourself.
— *Tibetan Proverb*

SEVENTEEN

Spiritual Science of Food

BHAGAVAD GITA
CHAPTER 17, VERSE 10

Yata yaman gata rasam
Puti paryusitam cha yat
Ucchistam api chamedhyam
Bhojanam tamasa-priyam

TRANSLATION

yata-yaman	food not freshly cooked	*api*	also
gata-rasam	tasteless	*chamedhyam*	and untouchable
puti	bad smelling	*bhojanam*	food
paryusitam	decomposed	*tamasa*	lethargic personality
ca	also	*priyam*	dear
yat	that which		
ucchistam	food eaten by others		

MEANING

Foods which are stale, without nutrition, putrid and impure are favoured by people with lethargic tendencies (not generally interested in spiritual matters).

Our Daily Bread

In our modern society, an ever increasing number of people are affected by obesity, diabetes and cardiovascular disease. It is important that we rethink how important our diet is for our health. If we take a minute and compare what we eat today to what our grandparents used to eat, we will observe major differences. Our great grandparents would have a difficult time recognizing many of the foods we consume on a daily basis nowadays. A big part of the problem is that fast food is affordable and served almost everywhere. The availability of highly processed food, and the ever growing consumption of junk food, have created severe health problems in recent years.

We consume huge quantities of industrialized food, and too little quantities of fresh vegetables and fruits. We eat a lot less fibre compared to the dietary fibre intake of our ancestors. Lately the quantity of dietary fibres that we consume daily has become smaller and smaller. But our human body did not have the required time to adapt itself to our modern nutrition and lifestyle. The change was fast, and it is speeding up without showing signs of slowing down.

If we continue to indulge in these bad eating habits we will destroy our chances of enjoying a healthy future. It seems that the major health problems that the future holds for us as a species are constipation, obesity and heart disease. If we want to avoid these, we need to go back to the basics and incorporate a lot of unprocessed and fresh foods into our diet. Eating more fruits and vegetables will assist in avoiding a lot of health problems. You will also lose weight, enjoy an active lifestyle and feel more energetic.

THE IMPORTANCE OF NUTRITION

Proper nutrition is important for our skin, brain, organs, immune system, lean body mass (LBM), metabolism or basal metabolic rate (BMR). Without a good meal plan, it would be very difficult to stay fit and healthy. A good nutritional plan gives the human body all the micro-nutrients (vitamins and minerals) and macro-nutrients (protein, fats and carbohydrates) it needs to survive. Without a correct balance of these nutrients, our body cannot function efficiently.

Nutrition is important in maintaining a healthy immune system. The human immune system is an amazing and complicated constellation of cells, organs, proteins, and tissues. All of these together work to respond to such foreign invaders as bacteria, viruses, fungi, and parasites, which can prove harmful and cause several diseases to your body. A unique thing about the immune system is that every cell and organ involved in it not only easily remember and identify millions of enemies that may attack your body, but also generate powerful chemical secretions in the form of fluid in order to get rid of all of them. The immune system plays an important role in protecting us from different kinds of diseases, from minor colds and flues to the most devastating ailments like cancer and heart diseases. Here are nine common foods to boost your immune system:

1. **Yogurt** – Sometimes acknowledged as miracle food, yogurt contains in it Lactobacillus acidophilus – a kind of healthy bacteria, which helps to fight infections as a result of virus, bacteria, and parasite germs.
2. **Garlic** – With a high content of phytochemicals and sulphuric compounds like allicin, garlic is considered highly effective as an immune booster and its intake helps to protect you from diseases

such as diabetes, heart disease, and cancer.

3. **Tumeric** – Enriched with therapeutic properties, turmeric's consumption helps to produce more immune cells.

4. **Green Tea** – it contains in it agents like epigallocatechin gallate (EGCG) that can fight bacteria and viruses. Green tea not only strengthens the immune system but also serves as an anti-cancer agent.

5. **Ginger** – Intake of ginger, especially with a cup of green tea, helps to boost the immune system by reducing the risk of developing cancers that affect the colon and ovaries.

6. **Sweet Potato** – It promotes a healthy immune system with its antioxidant properties and elements such as phytochemical carotene, which helps to strengthen bones, blood vessels, and tissues.

7. **Spinach** – Spinach is a good source of folate and antioxidants like quercetin that prevent many harmful viruses and bacteria from multiplying.

8. **Pumpkin** – A good source of essentials including Zinc and proteins. Eating pumpkin helps to strengthen the cells involved in the immune system.

9. **Oranges** – Their consumption helps to neutralize free radicals, as they contain powerful antioxidants in the form of Vitamin C.

Each person digests and assimilates food differently. In yogic science, the act of eating is considered to be a sacred act. This is based on the premise that a food item has to give up its own living existence in order for a human being to benefit from it. Food has the potential to nourish the body, the mind, and the spirit. For this gift, we should express gratitude at mealtime.

AYURVEDIC NUTRITION

Ayurveda, the 5000 year old medical system of India, takes the approach that poor nutrition is the main cause of disease. This ancient system uses food to heal and prevent illness. The primary problem with other nutritional approaches is that they are not orientated towards the individual using them. Modern nutrition uses a "one size fits all" approach for people of all different ages, sizes, shapes and cultures. Modern biochemical research from the 1950's has shown that each person's metabolism functions differently. Unfortunately, modern nutrition has no methodology to structure an individualized diet for each specific person.

For proper nutrition, care should be taken to insure that food be organic, fresh and whenever possible locally grown. In Ayurvedic science food, drinks, and spices are categorized according to their taste (sweet, salty, sour, bitter, pungent and astringent), the energetic effect they have on the **doshas**, as well as their post-digestive effect on the tissues. This is why when choosing foods it is important to understand our original constitution in order to eat foods that have the opposite qualities to those that are already predominant in the constitution. Furthermore, understanding the current state of the doshas is also crucial for making the right food choices.

Vata types tend to more deficient by nature and have light body frames, variable digestion and often have a tendency towards gas and constipation. Therefore, they do best eating warm, nourishing and primarily cooked foods, and should avoid dried, cold, frozen and excess intake of raw foods. Also, they should avoid pinto, garbanzo or black beans, which are hard to digest and tend to increase intestinal gas. Vata is balanced by sweet, sour and salty tasting foods.

Pitta types tend to have strong appetites and good digestion, but have a tendency toward hyperacidity and inflammatory disorders. So they should avoid eating greasy, hot spicy, salty and fermented foods, as well as sour and acidic fruits. Pitta is balanced by bitter, sweet and astringent tastes.

Kapha types are large framed with a tendency toward weight gain, obesity, sluggish digestion, lethargy and congestive disorders. They do best on a light, reducing diet low in carbohydrates and avoiding dairy, cold food and drinks, poor quality oils and sweet treats. Kapha is decreased with pungent, bitter and astringent tastes.

Another vital aspect of Ayurvedic nutrition is the manner in which food is combined. In Ayurveda, not all foods are compatible. In his 2004 article *Let your Food be your Medicine*, Vishnu Dass notes that certain foods, when eaten or cooked together, can disturb the normal function of the digestive fire and promote the accumulation of toxins in the body. Various factors, such as the tastes, qualities, and energies of certain foods, as well as how long they take to digest, affect how well certain foods will combine. Heavy foods such whole grains, dairy, meats and starches don't combine well with light foods such as fruit, which digest quicker. Another example is when sour and acidic fruits are combined with milk, which is sweet and cooling. This causes the milk to curdle and become heavy in the intestines, resulting in upset stomach. Ayurveda places great emphasis on the art of combining food for optimal nutritional benefit.

How you eat your meal is also important. The following are some general Ayurvedic guidelines for mealtime:

1. Steady the mind and the body before you begin to eat.

2. Begin your meal with a blessing.
3. Avoid eating when you are upset.
4. Avoid drinking ice-cold water with your meal. Sip warm water.
5. Serve freshly cooked food (within 3 hours of cooking) whenever possible.
6. Serve mostly cooked foods with small portions of salads of easily digestible carrots, cucumber and dark color greens.
7. Avoid serving milk with the meal. Milk is a hard food to digest and is best served by itself after it is warmed to make it more digestible. Milk is best served warm at night before going to bed.
8. Chew your food well.
9. Eat silently or have a pleasant conversation.
10. Eat a modest portion. Leave about 1/4 of the stomach empty to assist with digestion.
11. Rest a bit after the meal. Enjoy light conversation or relaxing music after the meal.

DISCUSSION QUESTIONS

1. Why are fast foods so harmful to our health?
2. What are the major challenges in changing eating habits?
3. How does an upset mind affect the digestion of food?
4. Why are spicy foods not recommended for pitta personality types?

INSPIRATIONAL QUOTES

The first wealth is health.
— *Emerson*

Our food should be our medicine
and our medicine should be our food.
— *Hippocrates*

He who takes medicine and neglects diet
wastes the skills of the physician.
— *Chinese Proverb*

The doctor of the future will no longer treat the human frame with
drugs, but rather will cure and prevent disease with nutrition.
— *Thomas Edison*

To eat is a necessity, but to eat intelligently is an art.
— *La Rochefoucauld*

When diet is wrong, medicine is of no use.
When diet is correct, medicine is of no need.
— *Ayurvedic Proverb*

Leave your drugs in the chemist's pot
if you can heal the patient with food.
— *Hippocrates*

EIGHTEEN

The Victorious Connection

BHAGAVAD GITA
CHAPTER 18, VERSE 78

Yatra yogesvarah krishno
Yatra partho dhanur dharah
Tatra srir vijayo bhutir
Dhruva nitir matir mama

TRANSLATION

yatra	where	tatra	there
yogeshwara	the Lord of Yoga	srih	success
krishno	Lord Krishna	vijayah	victory
yatra	where	bhutih	exceptional
partho	the son of Pritha, who is Arjuna		power
		dhruva	certain
dhanur dharah	who carries the bow and arrow, the archer	nitih	liberation
		matir mamamy	opinion

MEANING

Wherever there is Krishna, the Lord of Yoga, and Arjuna, the expert archer, there will certainly be success, victory, extraordinary powers and liberation. That is my opinion.

MEETING OF THE MINDS

This is the last verse of the *Bhagavad Gita*. The Song of the Lord concludes with a profound conviction from Sanjaya who has witnessed the divine conversation and the self realization of Arjuna. Sanjaya was blessed to be the information minister to the blind king Dhritarashtra so that he could observe the events at Kurukshetra and objectively report to the King. Based on his first hand experience, Sanjaya gives us his personal opinion which describes a very sacred contract between a human being and Divine Consciousness. This is the **sanathan dharma** – the eternal obligation of each human being.

The real value of the lesson in *Gita* is the awareness that there are the forces of the Kauravas and the Pandavas in each human being. This mere awareness allows us to create our own contingency plan to deal with situations when our not-so-nice side rears its head, and it will sometimes. This will happen in individual, family and social relationships. Sometimes we see a situation in which there is a remarkable career and/or financial success only to be undone by a specific addiction or weakness, which may appear quite out of character. In families also, we see admirable synergy and progress, and then the subsequent dismantling based on the jealousy or envy of one member. It is the force of the Kauravas asserting itself, often screaming for attention and expression. It may be as simple as the other side seeking attention and needing a forum and a voice to assert its presence. It is the law of duality. Today we have a number of psychoanalytical theories in humanistic psychology which explore this aspect of our personality.

The purpose of every life activity and experience is to move a human being inward and lead him/her back to an awareness of the

Divine Source. Two strong forces propel human life on Earth. In the *Gita*, Krishna tells Arjuna about the true Self, the forces of the mind, the correlation between thought and action and the universal Law of Karma. After explaining these concepts, he clearly says to Arjuna in the last Chapter:

> I have provided you with very important knowledge.
> Now Arjuna, reflect on this well and then do as you choose.
> – *Bhagavad Gita 18.63*

It is important to recognize that we shouldn't expect the Divine to suddenly appear and resolve all our problems by waving a magic wand. He or She could, but what would be the lesson in that? What experience would we gain? Krishna did not pick up a weapon and demolish the enemy forces like Rambo. He could have done so. Instead he remained in the Chariot as the charioteer and provided the advice and support for Arjuna to figure out his purpose and role on the battlefield. In doing so, the Divine is reminding us that Divinity lies in the hearts of all human beings. There is a drop in the ocean, and there is also an ocean in the drop. When we recognize this and make that connection, victory is assured.

Victory is a state of being where all possibilities exist and where we have the ability to manifest the desires of our heart and soul. Life on Earth offers us a network of endless possibilities. The battlefield symbolically represents the strife between vice and virtue within our own heart. The victory represents our ultimate triumph over our lower nature. This human life involves various battles, but the most important one is the battle within. We have no choice about fighting, but we do have a choice of which side to fight on.

HOPE AND ASSURANCE

There is a wonderful feeling of hope and optimism as we read the last verses of the *Bhagavad Gita*. Human beings are capable of remarkable change and progress in a positive forward direction. Wherever there is Krishna, or the presence of Divine Energy, it is possible to make great changes in the direction of our lives. We are made in the image of the Divine, and we all have that potential. In my career in the Criminal Justice System in Canada, I have seen the transformation that is possible when someone decides to turn their life away from sense gratification, impulsive actions and a life of pursuing criminal activities. Our role is not to judge the unfolding of karmic consequences in someone's life, but to provide the necessary support and encouragement as another fellow human being. We should do our part. Let God do the miracle of transformation.

We are provided with eighteen Chapters of the *Gita* documenting the initial reluctance of Arjuna to proceed with the battle. If we try to rationalize the hesitation, we can find a variety of reasons to justify that position. After his conversation with Krishna, Arjuna eventually realizes his potential and his purpose in life. In a similar manner, Uddhav realized his purpose in life and the specific behaviours required by someone on the spiritual path. This is explained in the following two verses in Canto 11, Chapter 14 of Shrimad Bhagawatam, in the Section known as the *Uddhav Gita*.

A devotee whose speech is sometimes choked up,
whose heart melts, who cries continually and sometimes laughs,

who feels ashamed and cries out loudly and then dances
- a devotee thus fixed in loving service to Me
purifies the entire universe.

Just as gold, when smelted in fire, gives up its impurities
and returns to its pure brilliant state, similarly,
the spirit soul, absorbed in the fire of bhakti-yoga,
is purified of all contamination caused by previous
fruitive activities and returns to its original position of
focusing on Me in the spiritual world.
– *Shrimad Bhagawatam 11.14. 24 - 25*

THE STORY OF NARAD

One day, the Indian sage Narad was walking with God across a vast desert. Narad turns to God and said, "God, what is the great secret of this life on Earth?" God smiles and remains silent. They continue walking.

"My dear Narad," God finally says "The sun is very hot today and I am thirsty. Straight ahead you will find a village. Could you please go there and get me some water?"

Narad sets off. Arriving at the village, he goes to the first house and knocks on the door. A beautiful young lady answers. The moment Narad looked into her eyes, he fell in love. She was remarkably beautiful with long, smooth, silky hair and lovely lips. Narad asks for some water and she invites him in. He is warmly welcomed by her family. It was as if everyone in this nice family had been expecting him.

It was supper time and Narad was asked to eat with the family and then to stay over for the night. He gladly accepts, enjoying the family's warm hospitality and secretly marvelling at the loveliness of the young woman. A week goes by, and then two weeks. Narad began to assist the family on the farm and then he asks to marry the beautiful young woman. The family was overjoyed and Narad married the young lady.

Narad and his young wife settled down in her family's home and they started a family. Over the next seven years they had three children – two sons and a daughter. The years go by. Soon, both his wife's mother and father pass on and Narad takes responsibility as the head of the household. He opened a small shop in the village and then another and started to employ some villagers. His business prospers. He became a well respected member of the community and was seen as a wise leader. Narad and his family lived happily for many years.

One evening, a violent storm started and it began to rain for several days. The nearby rivers rose and flooded their banks. The village soon started to flood. Narad gathers his family and leads them through the dark night to higher ground. But the storm will not let up. The winds increased in strength and one of Narad's sons is washed away. As Narad tries to grab his son, he lets go of his daughter and she is also washed away. The winds were fierce, and soon Narad lost his wife and his other son to the raging storm. Narad started to scream as he was tossed around by the winds. Then all goes black.

The next day, the storm eased up. Narad found himself washed up on to a sandbank far down the river. There was no sign of his family or anyone else. Bits of wreckage float pass him. He broke down in sorrow and abandonment and started to cry.

Narad hears a voice behind him. He turns around and there was

God. Suddenly, the river vanishes and once again Narad and God are in the empty desert.

"Where is my water?" asks God. Narad was speechless.

"Where is my water?" God asks again "I have been waiting for you."

Narad falls down before God. "I forgot," he cries "I forgot. I forgot what you asked me to do. Please forgive me."

God smiles and says "You are forgiven Narad. Now you understand the great secret of life on Earth. This world is an illusion. It's all maya."

FINAL COMMENTS

As I come to edit the final draft of this book, it is a lovely spring day in Edmonton, Alberta. The winter is over and change is in the air. As we now know, the United States Navy Seal commandos have just stormed a residence in Abbottabad, Pakistan and killed Osama Bin Laden. Approximately ten years ago, we witnessed the bombing of the World Trade Center in New York, an incident for which Bin Laden and the Al Qaeda supporters have proudly claimed responsibility, in addition to other terrorist incidents around the world. This was a different battlefield using modern communications technology, but it was still an important war, with adverse international consequences.

Money, political support, technology and networking can only go so far if our agenda is to cause human suffering on this Earth. We can rationalize our actions legally, politically, socially, economically and with religious rhetoric, but it does not provide a justified reason to endanger human life and create tears of suffering in the eyes of our fellow human beings. The day of accountability will come - sooner than we think! Here we are, an old man confined in a Pakistani home for years, dependent on the kindness of Mother Earth and the compassionate hearts of some fellow human beings. The Law of Karma is as effective as the Law of Gravity.

The lesson is clear. However wealthy or powerful you are, if you consciously choose to orchestrate the destruction of our fellow human beings, be careful. You may be comfortable in a palace, but the next knock on the door may not be room service!

COMING HOME

The souls of human beings are sent on Earth to play their role in the cosmic drama. We are all actors on this giant stage, but the divine component knows its home. The needle of a compass points northwards no matter which way the compass is turned.

Even after a long separation from his beloved, a lover is thrilled in body, mind and spirit as he contemplates the reunion with his sweetheart. Similarly, a yogi is thrilled with the thought of reconnecting with Divine Consciousness. Rumi describes this in his *Divani Shamsi Tabriz*:

> It is time to set out from this world.
> I hear a drum in my soul's ear
> coming from the depths of the stars.

The Bhagavad Gita is essentially the story of the soul's journey back to Source. It is a journey that each one of us must make. From the Chariot, Namaste!

INDEX

SUN SALUTATIONS
Surya Namaskar
Pranamasana
(Prayer Pose)
EXHALE

SUN SALUTATIONS
Surya Namaskar
Hasta Uttanasana
(Raised Arms Pose)
INHALE

2

SUN SALUTATIONS
Surya Namaskar Hastapaadasana (Standing Forward Bending Pose) **EXHALE**

SUN SALUTATIONS
Surya Namaskar
Ashwa Sanchalanasana
(Equestrian Pose)
INHALE

SUN SALUTATIONS
Surya Namaskar
Dandasana
(Four-Limbed Staff Pose)
EXHALE

SUN SALUTATIONS
Surya Namaskar
Ashtanga Namaskara (Salute with the Eight Limbs Pose)
HOLD

SUN SALUTATIONS
Surya Namaskar
Bhujangasana
(Cobra Pose)
INHALE

SUN SALUTATIONS
Surya Namaskar
Adho Mukha Svanasana
(Downward-Facing Dog)
EXHALE

SUN SALUTATIONS
Surya Namaskar
Ashwa Sanchalanasana
(Equestrian Pose; Lunge)
INHALE

SUN SALUTATIONS
Surya Namaskar
Hasta Uttanasana
(Raised Arms Pose)
INHALE

RECOMMENDED READING LIST

1. *The Bhagavad Gita: God talks with Arjuna* by Paramahansa Yogananda. Self Realization Fellowship, California 2005.

    Yogananda's commentary explains the wisdom of Lord Krishna's dialogue with Arjuna. Supported by modern scientific research, this book points to the science that supports universal spiritual principles and the yogic lifestyle.

2. *Danger: Truth at Work - The Courage to Accept the Unknowable* by Osho. OSHO Media International, Amsterdam 2010.

    A brilliant and provocative book that explores social conditioning and challenges the different aspects of our religious and social life.

Osho discusses pseudo-religions and the concept of the stick-on soul. He recommends a thorough dry cleaning of the human mind.

3. *The Hidden Messages in Water* by Masaru Emoto. Beyond Works Publishing Inc., 2004.

An amazing book documenting the experiments of Dr. Masaru Emoto, a Japanese scientist, who has shown that our words and thoughts have the power to change water and other substances.

4. *Light on Life: The Yoga Journey to Wholeness, Inner Peace and Ultimate Freedom* by B.K.S. Iyengar. Vancouver: Raincoast Books, 2005.

Written by the yoga master himself, this is an insightful and inspirational yogic journey into the physical, energy, mental, intellectual and divine components of the human body.

5. *Notes from The Universe: New Perspectives from an Old Friend* by Mike Dooley. Florida: Totally Unique Thoughts, 2003.

Sharing his experiences and discussing the wisdom of the Universe, Dooley focuses on the secret to manifesting personal change by engaging the power of the Universe.

6. *Anatomy of the Spirit: The Seven Stages of Power and Healing* by Caroline Myss. New York: Crown Publishers, 1996.

This book presents a wonderful picture of the energetic structure of the human body. Drawing on the wisdom traditions, the author shows that encoded within your body is an energy system which has access to the Divine Energy connecting all life.

7. *Bhagavad Gita As It Is* by A.C. Bhaktivedanta Swami Prabhupada. Los Angeles, California: International Society for Krishna Consciousness, 1994.

Written by the Vedic scholar and founder of ISKCON, this translation of *Gita* captures the deep devotional spirit of the bhakti movement and provides elaborate commentaries on the divine dialogue between Lord Krishna and Arjuna.

8. *Think on these Things* by Jiddu Krishnamurti. New York: Harper and Row Publishers Inc., 1970.

Structured in a Question and Answer format, this is a refreshing and thought provoking book which explores a variety of economic, social and cultural issues and examines our social and religious belief systems.

9. *Return to the Garden – A Journey of Discovery* by Shakti Gawain. Mill Valley, California: Nataraj Publishing, 1989.

The author describes her personal journey of discovery and the return to her authentic self, her connection to the Earth and a balanced way of life.

10. *Sambhog se Samadhi (From Sex to Super Consciousness)* by Osho. Amsterdam: Osho International Foundation, 2004.

This is the book that became world famous, and at the same time, world notorious.. Osho claims that there is a way to go beyond sex. You can transcend sex - you can use sex and erotic activity as a valuable tool for self-discovery and transformation. When sex becomes something sacred, not obscene, not pornographic and not repressed, but immensely respected, it can be used as our very life source in spiritual pursuits.

11. *The End of Sorrow: The Bhagavad Gita for Daily Living* by Eknath Easwaran. Berkeley, California: Blue Mountain Centre of Meditation, 1979.

The author discusses the ancient wisdom of the *Bhagavad Gita* and provides valuable commentaries for people to realize their real purpose and true potential in life.

12. *Krishna's Other Song: A New Look at the Uddhava Gita* by Steven J. Rosen. Connecticut: Praeger Publishers, 2010.

This book examines the esoteric teachings of *Uddhava Gita* in relation to other Vedic scriptures. It turns the spotlight on the background, philosophical dimensions and religious significance of Krishna's conversation with Uddhava.

13. *Hymns to an Unknown God: Awakening the Spirit in Everyday Life* by Sam Keen. New York: Bantam, 1994.

Keen invites us to explore new ways to transform the ordinary into the sacred. He addresses our current crisis of meaning and provides a blueprint for bringing spirituality into everyday life.

MANTRAS

A mantra is a powerful word or phrase. It comes from the Sanskrit word **mantram** which is a combination of the root word **manas** (mind) and **tram** (protection). A mantra literally means protection of the mind. The chanting of mantras like Om, depicted above, is popular in yoga and meditation classes as a way of centering oneself and preparing the mind for an introspective journey.

The chanting of mantras produce energy based sounds and physical vibrations in the body. Used with specific intentions, mantras create thought waves to energize and harmonize the mind and body. They are powerful conduits of spiritual energy used for healing, self development and manifestation. Repetition of a mantra is known as japa or mantra japa and it is usually done with a japa mala, a rosary consisting of 108 beads.

THE OLD YOGI AND HIS MANTRA

In India, the story is told of a young man who was a brilliant Sanskrit scholar. He was quite famous for his skills in memorizing and reciting various mantras. There was one mantra in particular where his recitation was impeccable.

One day he went to visit an old yogi who lived across the river in a small hut. He hired a boatman and they sailed over to meet the old yogi. As they shared some tea, the young man asked the yogi about his training and spiritual experiences. The old yogi said he didn't have much spiritual experience other than a particular mantra that he keeps repeating every day. As it turned out it was the same mantra that the young man knew quite well and had recited at several large gatherings.

As the old yogi chanted the mantra, the young man was horrified.

"What's wrong?" said the old yogi.

The young man replied "I don't know what to say. You are pronouncing the words of this mantra incorrectly! That is not how this mantra is chanted. I'm afraid you've wasted a lot of years repeating it the wrong way."

"Oh dear," said the old yogi "please tell me how it should be recited." So the young man taught the old yogi the proper way to recite the mantra.

Later that afternoon, they went out to sail along the river to enjoy the beautiful weather. The young man was thinking how fortunate that he came along to help this poor old yogi who may have never found out the correct way to recite that particular mantra.

"Excuse me please", said the old yogi, "I hate to bother you, but I have forgotten the correct pronunciation of that mantra. Could you repeat it again?" So the young man chanted the mantra again.

The old yogi slowly got up. Very slowly and very carefully he started to recite the mantra. Then he quietly stepped out of the boat and walked on the surface of the water back to his hut, leaving the young man and the boatman staring in amazement!

1. MAHA MANTRA - The Great Mantra

> Hare Krishna
> Hare Krishna
> Krishna Krishna
> Hare Hare
> Hare Rama
> Hare Rama
> Rama Rama
> Hare Hare

The Maha Mantra is special because it contains the names of the two most important incarnations of Lord Vishnu - Krishna and Rama. It is a direct and user friendly sixteen-word mantra for chanting in this fast paced modern world. Lord Vishnu is regarded as the aspect of Divine Consciousness that preserves life on Earth - hence his presence on Earth in different historical eras.

2. GAYATRI MANTRA – The Enlightenment Mantra

This is an ancient Vedic Mantra from the *Rig Veda* for illuminating the intellect. It is considered the mother of all mantras and is an effective vehicle for personal enlightenment.

ॐ भूर्भुवः स्वः
तत्सवितुर्वरेण्यं
भर्गो देवस्य धीमहि
धियो योनः प्रचोदयात् ।

Om
Bhur Bhuvah Suvah
That Savithur Varenyam
Bhargo Devasya Dheemahi
Dhiyo Yo Nah Prachodayath

Om	The primeval sound. It is known as "sarva rakshak", that which protects all.
Bhur	The physical world
Bhuvah	The mental world
Suvah	The spiritual world
That	that (The Divine Source)
Savithur	The Sun
Varenyam	most adorable
Bhargo	radiance
Devasya	The Supreme Lord
Dheemahi	we meditate upon
Dhiyo	the intellect
Yo	which (this Light)
Nah	our
Prachodayath	may it inspire

MEANING

We meditate upon the radiance of Supreme Lord who has created the physical, mental and spiritual worlds and is manifested as the adorable Sun. May this Light inspire our intellect.

3. THE RAMA HEALING MANTRA

This mantra has been used over the years to heal since Lord Rama is known as Dayasaraya, the Embodiment of Compassion.

> *Om Apadam Apahaartaram*
> *Dataram Sarva Sampadam*
> *Loka Bhi Ramam Sri Rama*
> *Bhuyo Bhuyo Namamyaham*

TRANSLATION

Om	the Universal sound
apadam	obstacles
apahaartaram	remover or destroyer
dataram	the giver
sarva sampadam	all wealth
lokabhiramam	one who pleases all people
Shri Rama	Lord Rama
bhuyo bhuyo	again and again
namamyaham	I bow

MEANING

I bow again and again to Lord Rama who removes obstacles, grants all wealth and pleases everyone.

Painting of Rama. South India, 1816.

4. SHANTI MANTRA – The Peace Mantra

This is a mantra from the *Brihadaranyaka Upanishad (Teachings of the Great Forest)*, which is used to bring a sense of peace and tranquility to a person.

> Om Asato Maa Sadgamaya
> Tamaso Maa Jyotir Gamaya
> Mrityor Maa Amritam Gamaya
> Ano badra kritawo yantu vishwata
>
> Om Shantih, Shantih, Shantih Om

MEANING

Lead me from unreal to real, lead me from darkness to light, and from death to immortality. Let noble thoughts come to me from everywhere. Let Peace prevail.

5. MANI MANTRA - The Jewel Mantra

Om (ohm)
Ma (mah)
Ni (nee)
Pad (padh)
Me (may)
Hum (hum)

MEANING
Hail the Jewel in the Lotus (*Mani* - Jewel, *Padma* - Lotus)

The Mani mantra is an important mantra in the Buddhist tradition. Its wisdom is universal. It salutes the jewel in the lotus - the inner divine wisdom or the spark of divinity in each human being. The lotus is a significant flower because it grows in the murky waters and yet produces a beautiful and fragrant flower, much like the human spirit rising from the polluted physical and mental environment. This mantra captures the whole objective of life - to seek, recognize and identify with the Divinity within each person.

6. Mantra for a Good Relationship

> OM
> Sahana Vavatu
> Sahana Bhunaktu
> Sahaveeryam Karavavahai
> Tejasvi Nau Adhitam Astu
> Ma Vidvishavahai
> Om Shanti Shanti Shanti

Translation

sahana	both of us	*nau*	us
vavatu	May He protect	*adhitam*	what is studied
sahana	both of us	*astu*	let it be
bhunaktu	May He nourish	*ma vidvishavahai*	may we not argue with each other
veeryam karavavahai May we acquire the capacity			
tejasvi	be brilliant	*shanti*	peace

Meaning

May He protect both of us. May He nourish both of us. May we both acquire the capacity to understand. May our study be brilliant. May we not argue with each other. Peace. Peace. Peace.

KIRTANS

Kirtan is a devotional practice and an important aspect of the path of Bhakti Yoga, the Yoga of Devotion. In the Ashtanga Yoga system, kirtan is categorized as pratyahara (withdrawal of the senses). Kirtan can be seen as a bridge between our outer and inner selves and an expression of our desire to know and love God within. Concentration on the different Names of the Divine, the meanings, or the ragas (melodic structures) increases the focus of the kirtan.

Kirtans are generally sung in a call and response style. The lead singer will sing a line and the group will respond by repeating that line. The speed increases and the drumming becomes faster in the later portion of the kirtan. The traditional musical instruments used in kirtan singing are the harmonium, dholak (two headed drum), tabla (a set of two separate drums), manjira (brass cymbals) and Ghatam (clay pot). The guitar, sitar, violin and keyboards are recent additions to the melody of kirtans.

For some, finding out the translation and meaning of the kirtan enhances concentration and devotion, while others prefer to dwell on the Name itself or on the beat. Concentration and focus are important aspects of singing kirtans. To this end, closing one's eyes, clapping, and listening intently both to the song and to changes in rhythm can help. Rhythm carries the energy of the kirtan. If the group is in sync, the atmosphere becomes charged with spiritual energy and the kirtan experience is enhanced.

Here are the lyrics of some simple kirtans:

1. SWAGATAM KRISHNA SHARANAGATAM KRISHNA

Swagatam Krishna Sharanagatam Krishna
Swagatam Su Swagatam Sharanagatam Krishna
Swagatam Krishna Sharanagatam Krishna

Mathurapuri Krishna Madhusudana Krishna
Swagatam Su Swagatam Sharanagatham Krishna
Swagatam Krishna, Sharanagatam Krishna

TRANSLATION

Swagatam	Welcome
su swagatam	heartfelt welcome
Sharanagatam	Welcome Home
Mathurapuri	City of Mathura
Krishna	Lord Krishna
Madhusudama	destroyer of Demon

2. SHREE KRISHNA GOVINDA

Chorus

Shree Krishna Govinda Hare Murari
Hey Nath Narayan Vasudeva

Hey Nath Narayan Vasudeva
Hey Nath Narayan Vasudeva (2)

Radhe Radhe, Krishna Krishna
Radhe Radhe, Krishna Krishna (2)

Hare Krishna, Hare Krishna
Krishna Krishna, Hare Hare (2)

3. GOPALA RADHA LOLA

Gopala, Radha Lola
Murali Lola Nandalala

Keshava Madhava Janardhana
Vanamala, Vrindavana Bala
Murali Lola Nandalala

Chant the name of the charming flute player,
Lord Krishna and the beloved Radha,
who walk the garden of Vrindavana with beautiful garlands.

4. KRISHNA KANAIYA BANSI BAJAIYA

Krishna Kanaiya Bansi Bajaiya
Para Karo Merey Jivana Naiya
Nandaji Key Lala Murali Gopala
Bhakto Key Tuma Dina Dayala
Para Karo Merey Jivana Naiya

Oh Lord Krishna, please help me cross the river of life and death.
Chant the names of Nanda and Gopala, the Lord of devotees.

5. JAI JAI RADHA RAMAN

Jai jai Radha Raman Hari Bol
Jai Jai Radha Raman Hari Bol

Vasudeva Sutan Devam, Kams Chaanur Mardanam
Devakee Paramanandam, Krishnam Vande Jagat Gurum

Mookam Karoti Vachaalam, Pangum Lamghayatee Girim
Yatkripa Tamaham Vande, Paramananda Maadhavam

6. HEY KRISHNA MADHUSUDANA

Govind, Hey Gopal, Hey Gopal
Keshava, Madhava, Hey Krishna Madhusudana,
Hey Krishna Madhusudana
Tere Khas Bandey, Khas Jalwa, Dekh lay tay hai, Dekh lay tay hai
Keshava, Madhava, Hey Krishna Madhusudana

7. GOPAL MURALIYA WALE

> *Jai Jai Shree Radhe*
> *Gopal Muraliya Wale*
> *Nandalall Muraliya Wale*
> *Hey Gopal, Hey Gopal, Hey Gopal*

The last two kirtans reverently invoke the different names of Lord Krishna (Gopal, Keshava, Madhava etc.) and glorify His special captivating Presence around humanity.

8. JAI HARI KRISHNA

> *Jai Hari Krishna, Jai Hari Krishna*
> *Govardhana Giridhaaree*
> *Radha Mohana Radha Jeevana*
> *Manjula Kunja Vihaaree*
>
> Victory to Lord Krishna.
> The one who lifted up the Goverdhana Mountain,
> and who was the life and joy of Radha.
> Hail to Lord Krishna who roamed the beautiful groves of Brindavana.

9. BHAJO KESHAVA HARI NANDALALA

Bhajo, Keshava Hari Nandalala
Bhajo Giridhari Gopala
Bhajo Shivashankar Gopala

Mathura may Hari janam liyo hai
Gokul jule Nandalala
Bhajo, Keshava Hari Nandalala

Jamuna kay gir dhenu charawe
Murali Bajaye Nandalala
Bhajo, Keshava Hari Nandalala

Meera Prabhu kay charan ki dasi
Sharanagat Pratipala
Bhajo, Keshava Hari Nandalala

Lord Krishna, dressed so beautifully
and playing your flute
on the banks of the Jamuna river.
We rock you in the cradle of our heart.

BIBLIOGRAPHY

Alexander, Samuel. *Space, Time and Deity, Volumes I & II.* Massachusetts: Peter Smith Publishers Inc., 1979.

Bansi, Pandit. *Hindu Dharma.* Illinois: B&V Enterprises Inc., 1996.

Chopra, Deepak. *Return of the Rishi: A Doctor's Search for the Ultimate Healer.* Boston: Houghton Mifflin, 1988.

Chopra, Krishan. *Your Life is in your Hands: The Path to Lasting Health and Happiness.* Boston: Element Books, 1999.

Desikachar, T.K.V. *The Heart of Yoga: Developing a Personal Practice.* Vermont: Inner Traditions, 1995.

Dyer, Wayne. *Inspiration: Your Ultimate Calling.* California: Hay House Inc., 2006.

Frawley, David. *Yoga and Ayurveda: Self Healing and Self Realization.* Wisconsin: Lotus Press, 1999.

Friedman, Lenore. *Meetings with Remarkable Women: Buddhist Teachers in America.* Boston: Shambhala, 1987.

Hansard, Christopher. *The Tibetan Art of Living: Wise Body, Mind, Life.* London: Atria Books, 2001.

Jung, Carl. *Modern Man in Search of a Soul.* New York: Harcourt, 1955.

Mitchell, Stephen, ed. *The Enlightened Mind: An Anthology of Sacred Prose.* New York: Harper Perennial, 1991.

Moore, Thomas. *Care of the Soul.* New York: Harper Collins, 1992.

Moody, Harry R. and Carroll, David. *The Five Stages of the Soul: Charting the Spiritual Passages that Shape our Lives.* New York: Doubleday, 1997.

Paramhansa, Yogananda. *The Second Coming of Christ: The Resurrection of the Christ Within You, Volumes I & II.* California: Self Realization Fellowship, 2004.

Perlmutter, Leonard with Perlmutter, Jenness Cortez. *The Heart and Science of Yoga: A Blueprint for Peace, Happiness and Freedom from Fear.* New York: AMI Publishers, 2005.

Powell, Barbara. *Windows into the Infinite.* California: Asian Humanities Press, 1996.

Redfield, James with Murphy, Michael and Timbers, Sylvia. *God and the Evolving Universe: The Next Step in Personal Evolution.* New York: Penguin Putman Inc., 2002.

Rumi, Jalaluddin. *The Essential Rumi, Translations by Coleman Barks and John Moyne.* San Francisco: Harper, 1995.

Shakti Kaur Khalsa. *Kundalini Yoga: The Flow of Eternal Power.* New York: Berkley Publishing, 1996.

Stapleton, Don. *Self Awakening Yoga: The Expansion of Consciousness through the Body's Own Wisdom*. Vermont: Healing Arts Press, 2004.

Tolle, Eckhart. *The Power of Now: A Guide to Spiritual Enlightenment*. California: New World Library, 1999.

Williamson, Marianne. *Everyday Grace: Having Hope, Finding Forgiveness and Making Miracles*. New York: Riverhead Books, 2002.

APPENDIX

FROM THE UDDHAV GITA
Lord Krishna Explains the Yoga System to Shri Uddhava

1. Sri Uddhava said: My dear Krishna, the learned sages who explain Vedic literature recommend various processes for perfecting one's life. Considering these varieties of viewpoint, my Lord, please tell me whether all these processes are equally important, or whether one of them is supreme.

2. My dear Lord, You have clearly explained the process of unalloyed devotional service, by which a devotee removes all material association from his life, enabling him to fix his mind on You.

3. The Supreme Personality of Godhead said: By the influence of time, the transcendental sound of Vedic knowledge was lost at the time of annihilation. Therefore, when the subsequent creation took place, I spoke the Vedic knowledge to Brahma because I Myself am the religious principles enunciated in the Vedas.

4. Lord Brahma spoke this Vedic knowledge to his eldest son, Manu, and the seven great sages headed by Bhrgu Muni then accepted the same knowledge from Manu.

5-7. From the forefathers headed by Bhrgu Muni and other sons of Brahma appeared many children and descendants, who assumed different forms as demigods, demons, human beings, Guhyakas, Siddhas, Gandharvas, Vidyadharas, Caranas, Kindevas, Kinnaras, Nagas, Kimpurusas, and so on.

All of the many universal species, along with their respective leaders, appeared with different natures and desires generated from the three modes of material nature. Therefore, because of the different characteristics of the living entities within the universe, there are a great many Vedic rituals, mantras and rewards.

8. Thus, due to the great variety of desires and natures among human beings, there are many different theistic philosophies of life, which are handed down through tradition, custom and disciple succession. There are other teachers who directly support atheistic viewpoints.

9. O best among men, the intelligence of human beings is bewildered by My illusory potency, and thus, according to their own activities and whims, they speak in innumerable ways about what is actually good for people.

10. Some say that people will be happy by performing pious religious activities. Others say that happiness is attained through fame, sense

gratification, truthfulness, self-control, peace, self interest, political influence, opulence, renunciation, consumption, sacrifice, penance, charity, vows, regulated duties or strict disciplinary regulation. Each process has its proponents.

11. All the persons I have just mentioned obtain temporary fruits from their material work. Indeed, the meager and miserable situations they achieve bring future unhappiness and are based on ignorance. Even while enjoying the fruits of their work, such persons are filled with lamentation.

12. O learned Uddhava, those who fix their consciousness on Me, giving up all material desires, share with Me a happiness that cannot possibly be experienced by those engaged in sense gratification.

13. One who does not desire anything within this world, who has achieved peace by controlling his senses, whose consciousness is equal in all conditions and whose mind is completely satisfied in Me finds only happiness wherever he goes.

14. One who has fixed his consciousness on Me desires neither the position or abode of Lord Brahma or Lord Indra, nor an empire on the earth, nor sovereignty in the lower planetary systems, nor the eightfold perfection of yoga, nor liberation from birth and death. Such a person desires Me alone.

15. My dear Uddhava, neither Lord Brahma, Lord Siva, Lord Sankarsana, the goddess of fortune nor indeed My own self are as dear to Me as you are.

16. With the dust of My devotees' lotus feet I desire to purify the material worlds, which are situated within Me. Thus, I always follow the footsteps of My pure devotees, who are free from all personal desire, rapt in thought of My pastimes, peaceful, without any feelings

of enmity, and of equal disposition everywhere.

17. Those who are without any desire for personal gratification, whose minds are always attached to Me, who are peaceful, without false ego and merciful to all living entities, and whose consciousness is never affected by opportunities for sense gratification—such persons enjoy in Me a happiness that cannot be known or achieved by those lacking such detachment from the material world.

18. My dear Uddhava, if My devotee has not fully conquered his senses, he may be harassed by material desires, but because of his unflinching devotion for Me, he will not be defeated by sense gratification.

19. My dear Uddhava, just as a blazing fire turns firewood into ashes, similarly, devotion unto Me completely burns to ashes sins committed by My devotees.

20. My dear Uddhava, the unalloyed devotional service rendered to Me by My devotees brings Me under their control. I cannot be thus controlled by those engaged in mystic yoga, Sankhya philosophy, pious work, Vedic study, austerity or renunciation.

21. Only by practicing unalloyed devotional service with full faith in Me can one obtain Me, the Supreme Personality of Godhead. I am naturally dear to My devotees, who take Me as the only goal of their loving service. By engaging in such pure devotional service, even the dog-eaters can purify themselves from the contamination of their low birth.

22. Neither religious activities endowed with honesty and mercy nor knowledge obtained with great penance can completely purify one's consciousness if they are bereft of loving service to Me.

23. If one's hairs do not stand on end, how can the heart melt? And if the heart does not melt, how can tears of love flow from the

eyes? If one does not cry in spiritual happiness, how can one render loving service to the Lord? And without such service, how can the consciousness be purified?

24. A devotee whose speech is sometimes choked up, whose heart melts, who cries continually and sometimes laughs, who feels ashamed and cries out loudly and then dances—a devotee thus fixed in loving service to Me purifies the entire universe.

25. Just as gold, when smelted in fire, gives up its impurities and returns to its pure brilliant state, similarly, the spirit soul, absorbed in the fire of bhakti-yoga, is purified of all contamination caused by previous fruitive activities and returns to its original position of serving Me in the spiritual world.

26. When a diseased eye is treated with medicinal ointment it gradually recovers its power to see. Similarly, as a conscious living entity cleanses himself of material contamination by hearing and chanting the pious narrations of My glories, he regains his ability to see Me, the Absolute Truth, in My subtle spiritual form.

27. The mind of one meditating upon the objects of sense gratification is certainly entangled in such objects, but if one constantly remembers Me, then the mind is absorbed in Me.

28. Therefore, one should reject all material processes of elevation, which are like the mental creations of a dream, and should completely absorb one's mind in Me. By constantly thinking of Me, one becomes purified.

29. Being conscious of the eternal self, one should give up association with women and those intimately associated with women. Sitting fearlessly in a solitary place, one should concentrate the mind on Me with great attention.

30. Of all kinds of suffering and bondage arising from various attachments, none is greater than the suffering and bondage arising from attachment to women and intimate contact with those attached to women.

31. Sri Uddhava said: My dear lotus-eyed Krishna, by what process should one who desires liberation meditate upon You, of what specific nature should his meditation be, and upon which form should he meditate? Kindly explain to me this topic of meditation.

32-33. The Supreme Personality of Godhead said: Sitting on a level seat that is not too high or too low, keeping the body straight and erect yet comfortable, placing the two hands on one's lap and focusing the eyes on the tip of one's nose, one should purify the pathways of breathing by practicing the mechanical exercises of puraka, kumbhaka and recaka, and then one should reverse the procedure (recaka, kumbhaka, puraka). Having fully controlled the senses, one may thus practice pranayama step by step.

34. Beginning from the Muladhara-Chakra, one should move the life air continuously upward like the fibers in the lotus stalk until one reaches the heart, where the sacred syllable om is situated like the sound of a bell. One should thus continue raising the sacred syllable upward the distance of twelve angulas, and there the Omkara should be joined together with the fifteen vibrations produced with anusvara.

35. Being fixed in the Omkara, one should carefully practice the pranayama system ten times at each sunrise, noon and sunset. Thus, after one month one will have conquered the life air.

36-42. Keeping the eyes half closed and fixed on the tip of one's nose, being enlivened and alert, one should meditate on the lotus flower situated within the heart. This lotus has eight petals and is situated on an erect lotus stalk. One should meditate on the sun, moon and fire, placing them one after the other within the whorl of that lotus flower. Placing My transcendental form within the fire, one should meditate upon it as the auspicious goal of all meditation. That form is perfectly proportioned, gentle and cheerful.

It possesses four beautiful long arms, a charming, beautiful neck, a handsome forehead, a pure smile and glowing, shark-shaped earrings suspended from two identical ears. That spiritual form is the color of a dark rain cloud and is garbed in golden-yellowish silk. The chest of that form is the abode of Srivatsa and the goddess of fortune, and that form is also decorated with a conch shell, disc, club, lotus flower and garland of forest flowers.

The two brilliant lotus feet are decorated with ankle bells and bracelets, and that form exhibits the Kaustubha gem along with an effulgent crown. The upper hips are beautified by a golden belt, and the arms are decorated with valuable bracelets.

All of the limbs of that beautiful form capture the heart, and the face is beautified by merciful glancing. Pulling the senses back from the sense objects, one should be grave and self-controlled and should use the intelligence to strongly fix the mind upon all of the limbs of My transcendental body. Thus one should meditate upon that most delicate transcendental form of Mine.

43. One should then pull the consciousness back from all the limbs of that transcendental body. At that time, one should meditate only on the wonderfully smiling face of the Lord.

44. Being established in meditation on the Lord's face, one should then withdraw the consciousness and fix it in the sky. Then giving up

such meditation, one should become established in Me and give up the process of meditation altogether.

45. One who has completely fixed his mind on Me should see Me within his own soul and should see the individual soul within Me, the Supreme Personality of Godhead. Thus, he sees the individual souls united with the Supreme Soul, just as one sees the sun's rays completely united with the sun.

46. When the yogi thus controls his mind by intensely concentrated meditation, his illusory identification with material objects, knowledge and activities is very quickly extinguished.

PERMISSIONS

Allegory of the Five Senses (page 17) by Gerard Lairesse. Public Domain.
Nervous System (page 142) © theEmirr. Licensed under the Creative Commons Attribution 3.0 Unported license.
Seven Chakras (page 165) © Peter Weltevrede
http://www.sanatansociety.com/indian_art_galleries/chakras.htm. Licensed under the Creative Commons Attribution-Share Alike 2.5 Generic license.
Lord Rama with Arrows (page 219) by Unknown. Public Domain.
"Om Mani Padme Hum" in Tibetan script (page 221) © Christopher J. Fynn. Licensed under the Creative Commons Attribution-Share Alike 3.0 Unported license.

ALSO BY THE AUTHOR

The Journey Inwards – A Simple Practical Guide to Personal Development. Edmonton, Alberta, 2000.
A short and simple booklet about the process of embarking on the journey of Personal Development.

Mandir Management – A Short Guide. Edmonton, Alberta, 2005.
A Workbook and Guide which offers practical ideas on the business of managing Mandirs in today's dynamic social and religious environment.

The Tulsi Project
An Ongoing Priority Project in Edmonton, Alberta which conducts research into the medicinal benefits of the Tulsi Plant (holy basil) and enhances public awareness of tulsi tea and essential oils through lectures and workshops.

www.ingramcontent.com/pod-product-compliance
Lightning Source LLC
Chambersburg PA
CBHW070641160426
43194CB00009B/1531